An illustrated

HISTORY
of the
WORLD

How we got to   where we are

GILLIAN CLEMENTS

Farrar, Straus and Giroux
New York

INTRODUCTION

I wanted to make a book which showed that history is both interesting and enjoyable – and I wanted it to be a history of the world and not just of one country or one race. I have chosen some of the most important developments in world history and described them in pictures and words (with a few jokes thrown in) in a way which I believe people of all ages can understand.

Choosing which facts to put in, and which to leave out, was difficult. Although this is a history of the world, many important events happened in Europe and in the United States which affected all of us. For example, for several hundred years after the explorations of the sixteenth century, a small number of countries had worldwide influence through their trade, their empires, and their dominance in science and technology. These events had to be included.

The lives of people across the world are changing more quickly today than at any time in the past: printing, radio, and television have transformed the communication of ideas, facts, and propaganda; new sources of energy and new ways of manufacturing have brought problems in their wake which affect us all; and, sadly, there are still wars and revolutions being fought. By learning about the past we can help ourselves toward an understanding of the problems of today and tomorrow. History can be as exciting, extraordinary, and dramatic as any work of fiction. I hope this book may encourage you to read and find out more about the history of men and women and of our planet.

Gillian Clements

CONTENTS

THERE IS A HISTORY IN ALL MEN'S LIVES

JUST A PEER AMID THE RUINS.

COUGH!

LOOKING FOR SOMETHING?

In the Beginning

All dates approximate

There are several theories for the ORIGIN OF THE UNIVERSE.

The temperature of the BIG BANG was more 100 billion degrees Celsius.

THE BIG BANG THEORY The Big Bang was an explosion of tremendous energy which happened 15 billion years ago.

This is why the universe is still expanding.

Energy and matter were hurled outward to make new galaxies.

The BIG BANG!

THE OSCILLATING UNIVERSE THEORY says that the universe is continually expanding, then contracting. After contracting, there is a BIG BANG, causing another expansion.

BANG!

BANG!

BANG!

AAGH!

JUMP!

EEEK!

JUMP!

NOTHING EVER HAPPENS AROUND HERE.

YAWN

BORING ISN'T IT

THE STEADY STATE THEORY says that the universe will go on forever, and that it did not start with a BIG BANG.

The Earth is not round; it bulges out around the Equator.

COUGH! SPLUTTER!

Early on, the Earth's atmosphere may have included carbon dioxide, nitrogen, methane, hydrogen, and water vapor; but NO OXYGEN!

THE EARTH

4½ billion years ago, the Earth was made from the material of a solar nebula (a cloud of dust and gases) which contracted to a hot core. As it cooled, a crust formed on the outside. Around 3½ billion years ago, a thin layer of atmosphere began to form around the Earth.

the atmosphere

SQUELCH!

SLOSH!

Primordial Soup

About 3 billion years ago, primitive life, like bacteria and blue-green algae, came from the organic compounds made from gases dissolving in the sea.

QUICK-EVOLVING HIGH-ABSORBING

PRIMORDIAL SOUP

The first primitive living organisms fed off a primordial soup, a dilute mixture of nutrients.

There are lots of different sorts of stars in the galaxy, including red giants, white dwarfs, and black holes.

COME IN, THE WATER'S LOVELY!

Steam from volcanic eruptions had turned into rain, and the rain had helped make the seas.

Animals, plants, and, later, humans on each continent isolated from one another

They began to adapt and evolve differently

'BYE!

From about 200 to 180 million years ago, one huge land mass called **PANGAEA** split in two, to make **LAURASIA** (today's N. America, Europe, and Asia) and **GONDWANALAND** (Africa, S. America, India, Antarctica, and Australia). They split again to make today's continents.

6

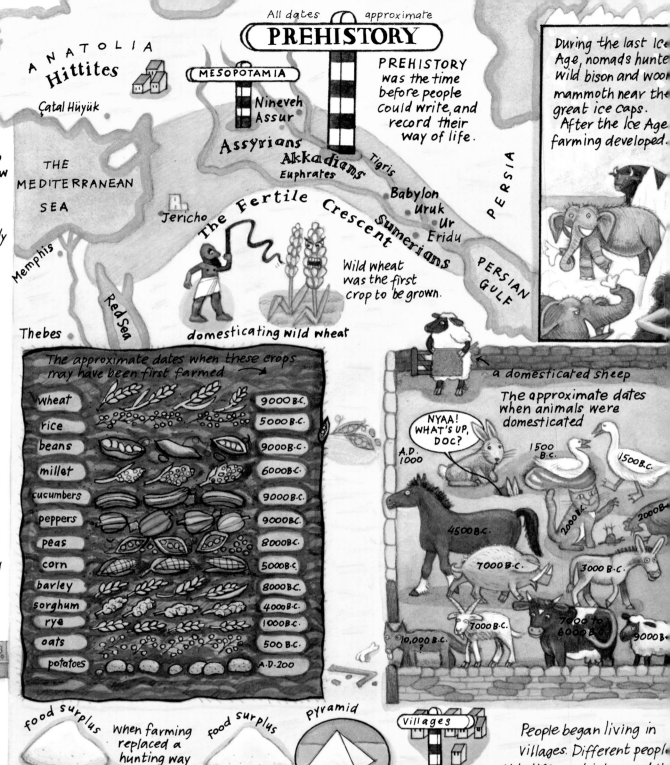

PREHISTORY

In the Fertile Crescent there were rich soils in the valleys of the rivers Tigris and Euphrates.

Around 9000 years B.C., New Stone Age (Neolithic) hunters and gatherers slowly changed their way of life by growing crops and keeping animals for meat, milk, skins, or wool.

BUT!

Some people think that farming began in southeast Asia, not the Fertile Crescent. 10,000 years ago, grains and vegetables were grown there.

Carbon dating can tell us how old crops and man-made objects are.

AT THE END OF THE ICE AGE

PREHISTORY was the time before people could write, and record their way of life.

A N A T O L I A
Hittites
Çatal Hüyük

MESOPOTAMIA
Nineveh
Assur
Assyrians
Akkadians
Euphrates

THE MEDITERRANEAN SEA

Memphis

Jericho

The Fertile Crescent

Tigris

Babylon
Uruk
Ur
Eridu
Sumerians

P E R S I A

PERSIAN GULF

Red Sea

Thebes

domesticating wild wheat

Wild wheat was the first crop to be grown.

During the last Ice Age, nomads hunted wild bison and woolly mammoth near the great ice caps.

After the Ice Age farming developed.

a domesticated sheep

The approximate dates when these crops may have been first farmed

wheat	9000 B.C.
rice	5000 B.C.
beans	9000 B.C.
millet	6000 B.C.
cucumbers	9000 B.C.
peppers	9000 B.C.
peas	8000 B.C.
corn	5000 B.C.
barley	8000 B.C.
sorghum	4000 B.C.
rye	1000 B.C.
oats	500 B.C.
potatoes	A.D. 200

The approximate dates when animals were domesticated

NYAA! WHAT'S UP, DOC?

A.D. 1000
1500 B.C.
1500 B.C.
2000 B.C.
2000 B.C.
4500 B.C.
7000 B.C.
3000 B.C.
10,000 B.C.?
7000 B.C.
7000 to 6000 B.C.
9000 B.C.

food surplus

When farming replaced a hunting way of life, not everyone was needed to help grow food crops.

food surplus

Pyramid

Some people were free to do other things, like designing pyramids!

Villages

People began living in villages. Different people did different jobs, and the villages soon grew into CITIES.

9000 Years B.C. Agriculture develops in the Fertile Crescent and Asia.

8000 Jericho is a city of 2000 people.

7000 Pottery, spinning, weaving, and metalwork develop in Mesopotamia.

6000 Çatal Hüyük is a city of over 5000 people. Farming developed in Central and South America

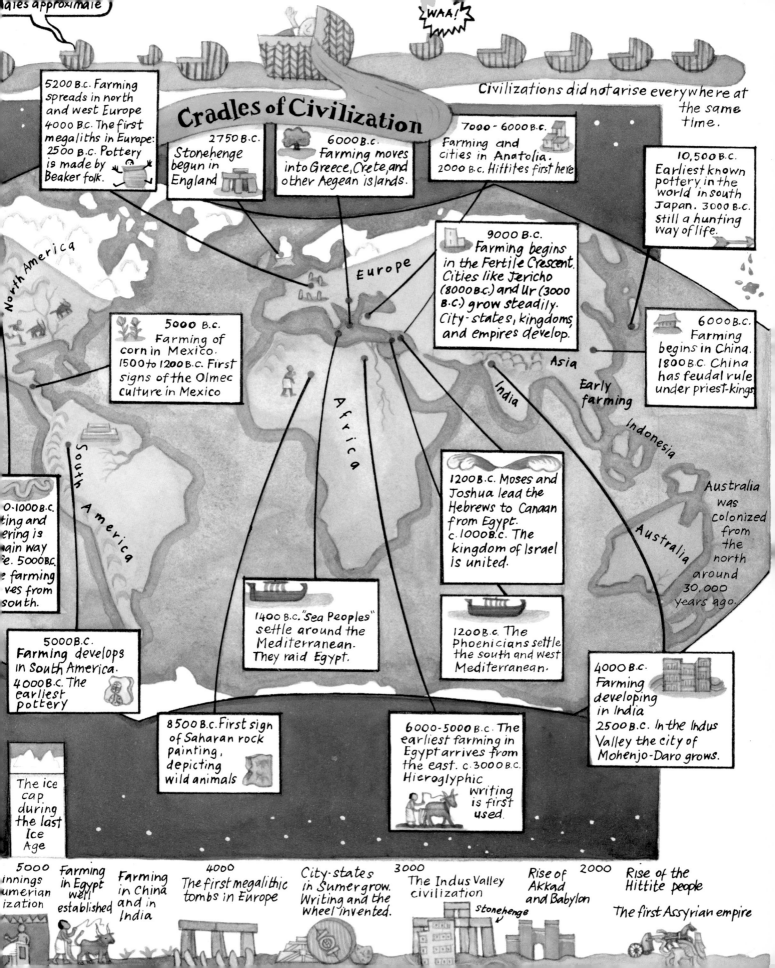

Cradles of Civilization

ales approximate

WAA!

Civilizations did not arise everywhere at the same time.

5200 B.C. Farming spreads in north and west Europe. **4000 B.C.** The first megaliths in Europe. **2500 B.C.** Pottery is made by Beaker folk.

2750 B.C. Stonehenge begun in England.

6000 B.C. Farming moves into Greece, Crete, and other Aegean islands.

7000 - 6000 B.C. Farming and cities in Anatolia. **2000 B.C.** Hittites first here.

10,500 B.C. Earliest known pottery in the world in south Japan. **3000 B.C.** still a hunting way of life.

9000 B.C. Farming begins in the Fertile Crescent. Cities like Jericho (8000 B.C.) and Ur (3000 B.C.) grow steadily. City-states, kingdoms, and empires develop.

6000 B.C. Farming begins in China. **1800 B.C.** China has feudal rule under priest-kings.

5000 B.C. Farming of corn in Mexico. **1500 to 1200 B.C.** First signs of the Olmec culture in Mexico.

North America

Europe

Asia

India

Early farming

Indonesia

Africa

South America

...0-1000 B.C. ...ting and ...ering is ...ain way ...e. 5000 B.C. ...e farming ...ves from ...south.

1200 B.C. Moses and Joshua lead the Hebrews to Canaan from Egypt. **c.1000 B.C.** The kingdom of Israel is united.

Australia was colonized from the north around 30,000 years ago.

Australia

1400 B.C. "Sea Peoples" settle around the Mediterranean. They raid Egypt.

1200 B.C. The Phoenicians settle the south and west Mediterranean.

5000 B.C. Farming develops in South America. **4000 B.C.** The earliest pottery.

8500 B.C. First sign of Saharan rock painting, depicting wild animals.

6000-5000 B.C. The earliest farming in Egypt arrives from the east. **c.3000 B.C.** Hieroglyphic writing is first used.

4000 B.C. Farming developing in India. **2500 B.C.** In the Indus Valley the city of Mohenjo-Daro grows.

The ice cap during the last Ice Age

5000 ...innings ...umerian ...ization

Farming in Egypt well established

Farming in China and in India

4000 The first megalithic tombs in Europe

City-states in Sumer grow. Writing and the wheel invented.

3000 The Indus Valley civilization

Stonehenge

Rise of Akkad and Babylon

2000 Rise of the Hittite people

The first Assyrian empire

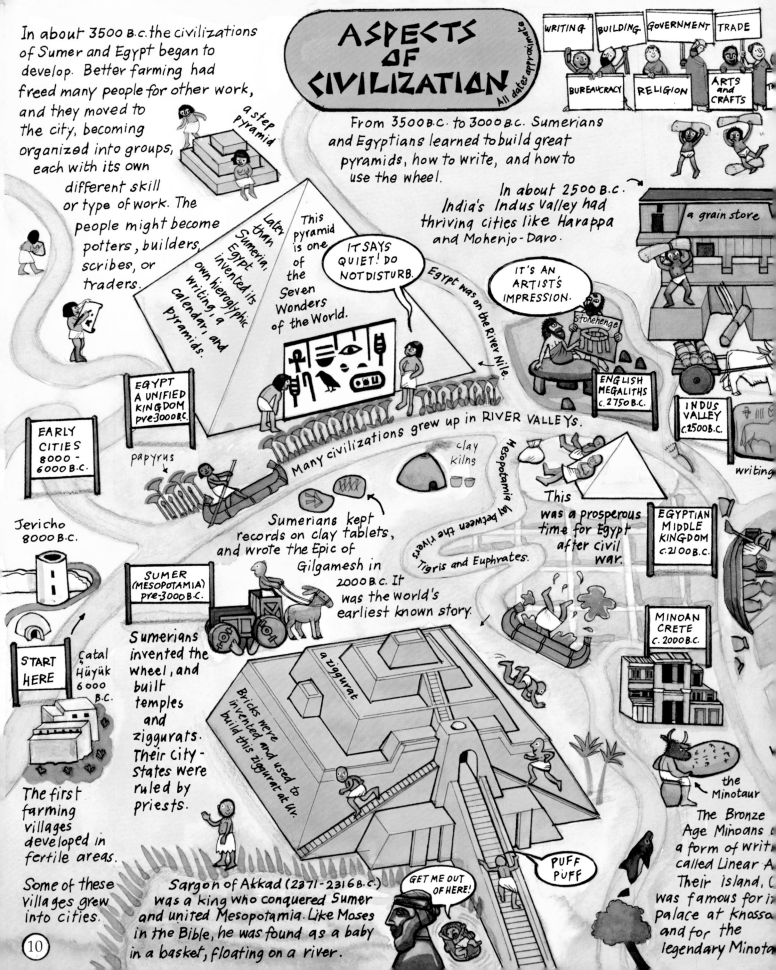

In about 3500 B.C. the civilizations of Sumer and Egypt began to develop. Better farming had freed many people for other work, and they moved to the city, becoming organized into groups, each with its own different skill or type of work. The people might become potters, builders, scribes, or traders.

a step pyramid

ASPECTS OF CIVILIZATION
All dates approximate

WRITING BUILDING GOVERNMENT TRADE
BUREAUCRACY RELIGION ARTS and CRAFTS

From 3500 B.C. to 3000 B.C. Sumerians and Egyptians learned to build great pyramids, how to write, and how to use the wheel.

In about 2500 B.C. India's Indus Valley had thriving cities like Harappa and Mohenjo-Daro.

a grain store

Later than Sumeria, Egypt invented its own hieroglyphic writing, a calendar, and Pyramids.

This pyramid is one of the Seven Wonders of the World.

IT SAYS QUIET! DO NOT DISTURB.

Egypt was on the River Nile.

IT'S AN ARTIST'S IMPRESSION.

Stonehenge

ENGLISH MEGALITHS c. 2750 B.C.

INDUS VALLEY c. 2500 B.C.

EGYPT A UNIFIED KINGDOM pre-3000 B.C.

papyrus

EARLY CITIES 8000 - 6000 B.C.

Jericho 8000 B.C.

Many civilizations grew up in RIVER VALLEYS.

clay kilns

writing

Sumerians kept records on clay tablets, and wrote the Epic of Gilgamesh in 2000 B.C. It was the world's earliest known story.

Mesopotamia lay between the rivers Tigris and Euphrates.

This was a prosperous time for Egypt after civil war.

EGYPTIAN MIDDLE KINGDOM c. 2100 B.C.

SUMER (MESOPOTAMIA) pre-3000 B.C.

Sumerians invented the wheel, and built temples and ziggurats. Their city-states were ruled by priests.

MINOAN CRETE c. 2000 B.C.

START HERE

Çatal Hüyük 6000 B.C.

The first farming villages developed in fertile areas.

a ziggurat

Bricks were invented and used to build this ziggurat at Ur.

the Minotaur

Some of these villages grew into cities.

Sargon of Akkad (2371-2316 B.C.) was a king who conquered Sumer and united Mesopotamia. Like Moses in the Bible, he was found as a baby in a basket, floating on a river.

GET ME OUT OF HERE!

PUFF PUFF

The Bronze Age Minoans [...] a form of writ[...] called Linear A[...] Their island, C[...] was famous for i[...] palace at Knossa[...] and for the legendary Minota[...]

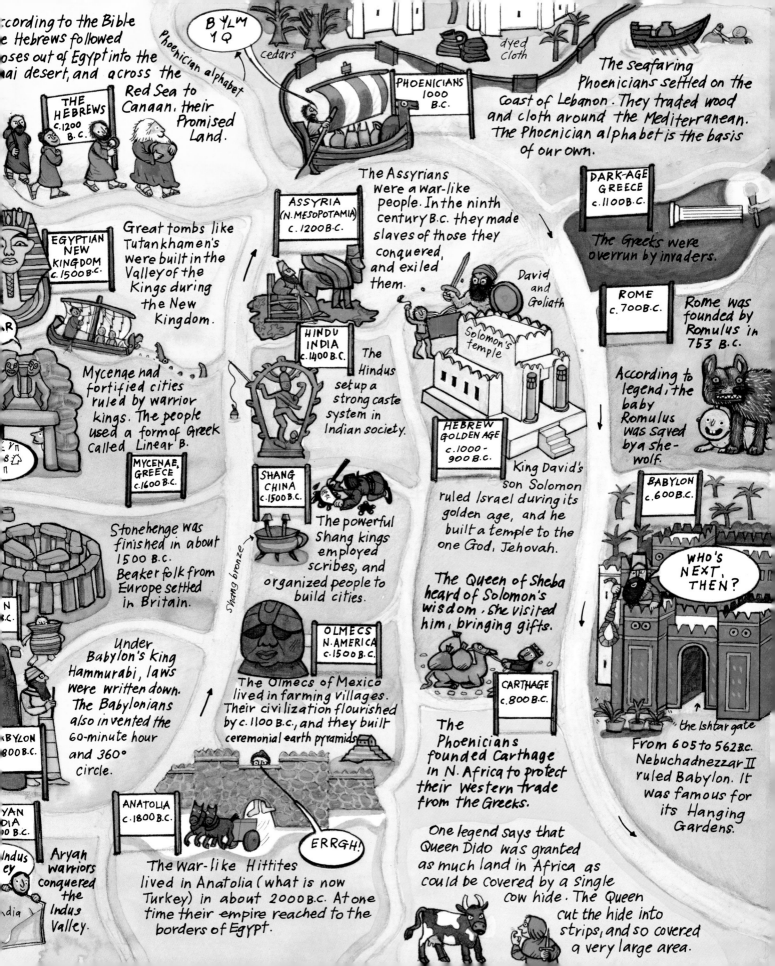

According to the Bible the Hebrews followed Moses out of Egypt into the Sinai desert, and across the Red Sea to Canaan, their Promised Land.

THE HEBREWS c.1200 B.C.

Phoenician alphabet

B Y L M 1 Q

cedars

dyed cloth

PHOENICIANS 1000 B.C.

The seafaring Phoenicians settled on the coast of Lebanon. They traded wood and cloth around the Mediterranean. The Phoenician alphabet is the basis of our own.

EGYPTIAN NEW KINGDOM c.1500 B.C.

Great tombs like Tutankhamen's were built in the Valley of the Kings during the New Kingdom.

ASSYRIA (N.MESOPOTAMIA) c.1200 B.C.

The Assyrians were a war-like people. In the ninth century B.C. they made slaves of those they conquered, and exiled them.

DARK-AGE GREECE c.1100 B.C.

The Greeks were overrun by invaders.

ROME c.700 B.C.

Rome was founded by Romulus in 753 B.C.

David and Goliath

Solomon's temple

HEBREW GOLDEN AGE c.1000 - 900 B.C.

According to legend, the baby Romulus was saved by a she-wolf.

Mycenae had fortified cities ruled by warrior kings. The people used a form of Greek called Linear B.

MYCENAE, GREECE c.1600 B.C.

HINDU INDIA c.1400 B.C.

The Hindus set up a strong caste system in Indian society.

SHANG CHINA c.1500 B.C.

Shang bronze

The powerful Shang kings employed scribes, and organized people to build cities.

King David's son Solomon ruled Israel during its golden age, and he built a temple to the one God, Jehovah.

BABYLON c.600 B.C.

Stonehenge was finished in about 1500 B.C. Beaker folk from Europe settled in Britain.

The Queen of Sheba heard of Solomon's wisdom. She visited him, bringing gifts.

WHO'S NEXT, THEN?

Under Babylon's king Hammurabi, laws were written down. The Babylonians also invented the 60-minute hour and 360° circle.

OLMECS N.AMERICA c.1500 B.C.

The Olmecs of Mexico lived in farming villages. Their civilization flourished by c.1100 B.C., and they built ceremonial earth pyramids.

CARTHAGE c.800 B.C.

The Phoenicians founded Carthage in N. Africa to protect their western trade from the Greeks.

the Ishtar gate

From 605 to 562 B.C. Nebuchadnezzar II ruled Babylon. It was famous for its Hanging Gardens.

BABYLON 1800 B.C.

ANATOLIA c.1800 B.C.

ERRGH!

The War-like Hittites lived in Anatolia (what is now Turkey) in about 2000 B.C. At one time their empire reached to the borders of Egypt.

Aryan warriors conquered the Indus Valley.

One legend says that Queen Dido was granted as much land in Africa as could be covered by a single cow hide. The Queen cut the hide into strips, and so covered a very large area.

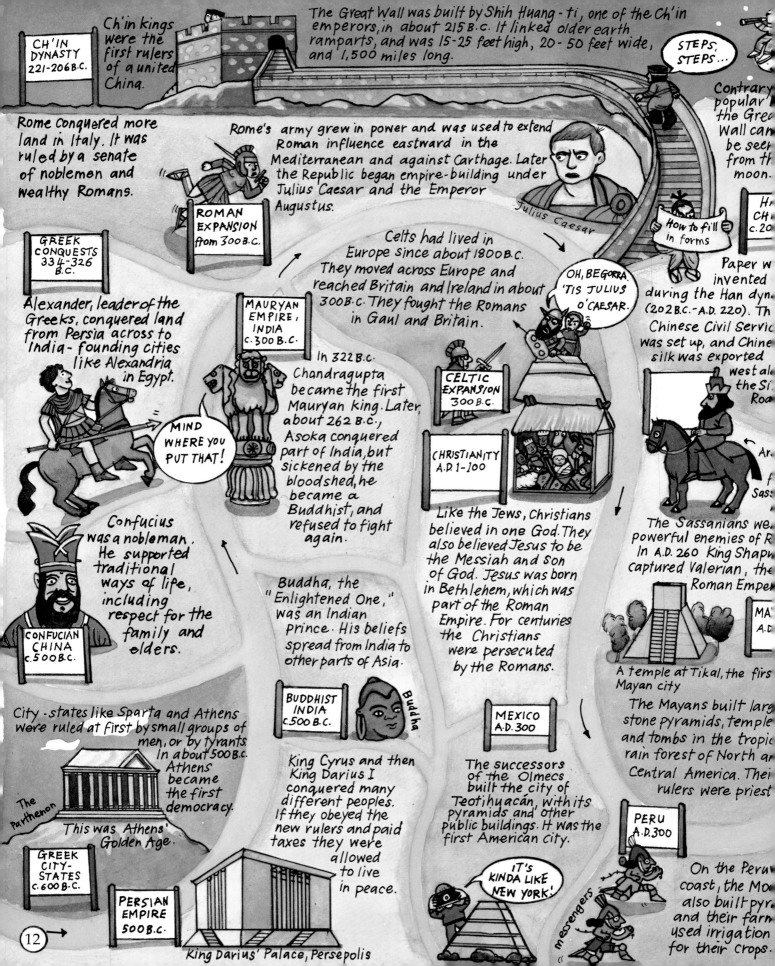

Ch'in kings were the first rulers of a united China.

The Great Wall was built by Shih Huang-ti, one of the Ch'in emperors, in about 215 B.C. It linked older earth ramparts, and was 15-25 feet high, 20-50 feet wide, and 1,500 miles long.

STEPS, STEPS...

Contrary popular the Grea Wall can be seer from th moon.

Rome conquered more land in Italy. It was ruled by a senate of noblemen and wealthy Romans.

Rome's army grew in power and was used to extend Roman influence eastward in the Mediterranean and against Carthage. Later the Republic began empire-building under Julius Caesar and the Emperor Augustus.

Julius Caesar

How to fill in forms

H CH c. 20

Paper w invented during the Han dyn (202 B.C.-A.D. 220). Th Chinese Civil Servic was set up, and Chine silk was exported west al the Si Roa

ROMAN EXPANSION from 300 B.C.

GREEK CONQUESTS 334-326 B.C.

Alexander, leader of the Greeks, conquered land from Persia across to India - founding cities like Alexandria in Egypt.

MIND WHERE YOU PUT THAT!

MAURYAN EMPIRE, INDIA c. 300 B.C.

Celts had lived in Europe since about 1800 B.C. They moved across Europe and reached Britain and Ireland in about 300 B.C. They fought the Romans in Gaul and Britain.

OH, BEGORRA 'TIS JULIUS O'CAESAR.

CELTIC EXPANSION 300 B.C.

In 322 B.C. Chandragupta became the first Mauryan king. Later, about 262 B.C., Asoka conquered part of India, but sickened by the bloodshed, he became a Buddhist, and refused to fight again.

CHRISTIANITY A.D. 1-100

Like the Jews, Christians believed in one God. They also believed Jesus to be the Messiah and Son of God. Jesus was born in Bethlehem, which was part of the Roman Empire. For centuries the Christians were persecuted by the Romans.

The Sassanians we. powerful enemies of R In A.D. 260 King Shapu captured Valerian, the Roman Emper

Ar f Sass

MA A.D

Confucius was a nobleman. He supported traditional ways of life, including respect for the family and elders.

CONFUCIAN CHINA c. 500 B.C.

Buddha, the "Enlightened One," was an Indian prince. His beliefs spread from India to other parts of Asia.

A temple at Tikal, the firs Mayan city

The Mayans built larg stone pyramids, temple and tombs in the tropic rain forest of North ar Central America. Thei rulers were priest

City-states like Sparta and Athens were ruled at first by small groups of men, or by tyrants. In about 500 B.C. Athens became the first democracy.

The Parthenon

This was Athens' Golden Age.

BUDDHIST INDIA c. 500 B.C.

Buddha

MEXICO A.D. 300

The successors of the Olmecs built the city of Teotihuacán, with its pyramids and other public buildings. It was the first American city.

PERU A.D. 300

On the Peru coast, the Mo also built pyr and their farm used irrigation for their crops.

GREEK CITY-STATES c. 600 B.C.

King Cyrus and then King Darius I conquered many different peoples. If they obeyed the new rulers and paid taxes they were allowed to live in peace.

PERSIAN EMPIRE 500 B.C.

King Darius' Palace, Persepolis

IT'S KINDA LIKE NEW YORK!

messengers

THE HISTORICAL RECORD

When writing was invented, it marked the end of prehistoric times, and the beginning of the recording of men's and women's lives. Before this, we could not be sure what had happened in the past. Writing lets us know.

Sumerians baked the clay tablet to make the writing on it permanent.

Sumerian Cuneiform writing

Writing was very important to early civilizations because it made it easier to record such important things as laws and taxes.
Writing began in Sumeria about 3000 B.C. with a form of picture writing. Tax records were written with reed pens on soft clay, and this wedge-shaped picture writing is called CUNEIFORM.

Soon after, in ancient Egypt, a different picture writing called HIEROGLYPHICS was invented. Scribes carved it in stone on tombs and other buildings or wrote it on papyrus with pen and ink. Papyrus was a paper made from strips of reed pith pounded together. It was a good surface to write on, and the papyrus could be made into a roll.

!@!

A scribe and (above him) the Egyptian symbol for a scribe

Thoth, the Scribe God

The first ALPHABET was a great breakthrough. Each letter represented a sound. The first alphabets we know about are used in Hebrew, Arabic, and Phoenician writing.
Our own alphabet comes from the Greek which was copied from the Phoenician.

 a Phoenician A
 a Greek A
A a Roman A

Sumerian

Indus Valley

Minoan Linear A (Crete)

Greek
ΔΡΟΣ

Hebrew

Chinese

BEWARE!

I, King Erk of Eridu, Emperor of the World, Master of the Universe, champion goat-eye juggler of Sumer, and professional shrimp-wrestler...

The historical record does not always tell the whole truth: find out who has written it and WHY!

COULD HE BE LYING?

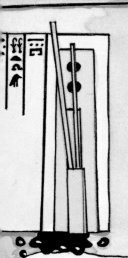

Egyptian

SOME EARLY FORMS OF WRITING AROUND THE WORLD

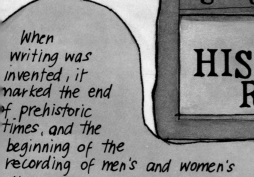

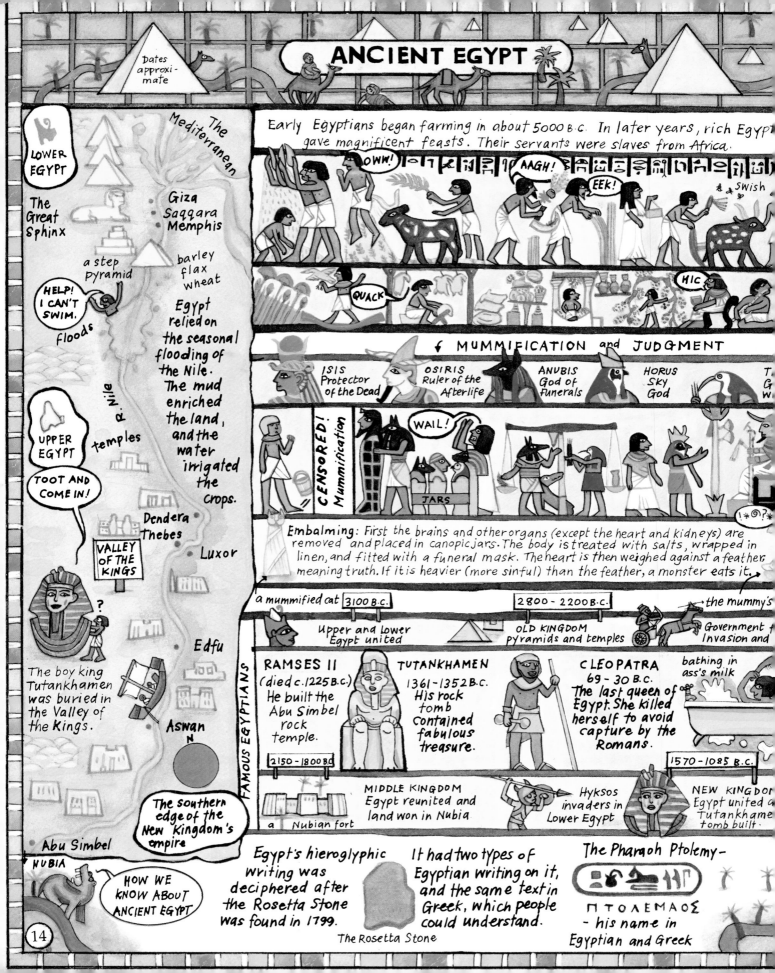

Dates approximate

LOWER EGYPT

The Mediterranean

The Great Sphinx

Giza
Saqqara
Memphis

a step pyramid

barley
flax
wheat

HELP! I CAN'T SWIM.

floods

Egypt relied on the seasonal flooding of the Nile. The mud enriched the land, and the water irrigated the crops.

R. Nile

UPPER EGYPT

temples

TOOT AND COME IN!

Dendera
Thebes

VALLEY OF THE KINGS

Luxor

?

The boy king Tutankhamen was buried in the Valley of the Kings.

Edfu

Aswan

N

The southern edge of the New Kingdom's empire

Abu Simbel

NUBIA

HOW WE KNOW ABOUT ANCIENT EGYPT

Early Egyptians began farming in about 5000 B.C. In later years, rich Egypt gave magnificent feasts. Their servants were slaves from Africa.

OWW!
AAGH!
EEK!
Swish
QUACK
HIC

MUMMIFICATION and JUDGMENT

ISIS Protector of the Dead
OSIRIS Ruler of the Afterlife
ANUBIS God of Funerals
HORUS Sky God
T G W

CENSORED! Mummification

WAIL!

JARS

Embalming: First the brains and other organs (except the heart and kidneys) are removed and placed in canopic jars. The body is treated with salts, wrapped in linen, and fitted with a funeral mask. The heart is then weighed against a feather meaning truth. If it is heavier (more sinful) than the feather, a monster eats it.

a mummified cat | 3100 B.C. | 2800 - 2200 B.C. | the mummy's

Upper and Lower Egypt united

OLD KINGDOM pyramids and temples

Government Invasion and

FAMOUS EGYPTIANS

RAMSES II (died c. 1225 B.C.) He built the Abu Simbel rock temple.

TUTANKHAMEN 1361 - 1352 B.C. His rock tomb contained fabulous treasure.

CLEOPATRA 69 - 30 B.C. The last queen of Egypt. She killed herself to avoid capture by the Romans.

bathing in ass's milk

2150 - 1800 B.C.

1570 - 1085 B.C.

a Nubian fort

MIDDLE KINGDOM Egypt reunited and land won in Nubia

Hyksos invaders in Lower Egypt

NEW KINGDOM Egypt united Tutankhamen tomb built

Egypt's hieroglyphic writing was deciphered after the Rosetta Stone was found in 1799.

The Rosetta Stone

It had two types of Egyptian writing on it, and the same text in Greek, which people could understand.

The Pharaoh Ptolemy-

ΠΤΟΛΕΜΑΟΣ - his name in Egyptian and Greek

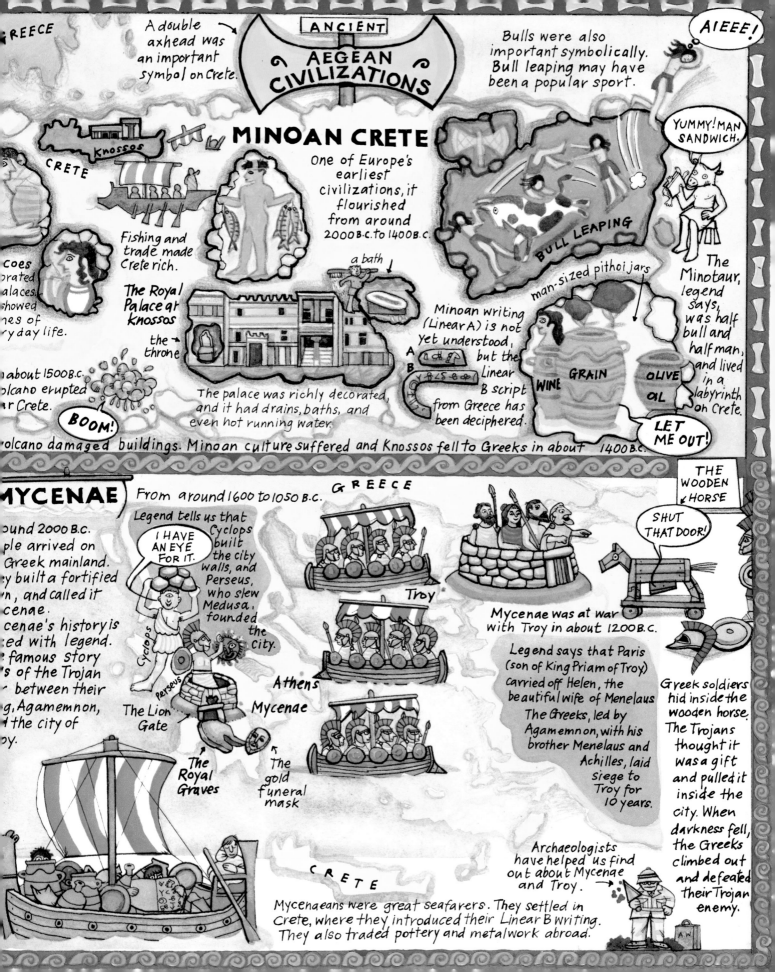

GODS and GODDESSES

POSEIDON · GOD OF THE SEA · APOLLO · GOD OF THE SUN · HERA · QUEEN OF HEAVEN · ZEUS · KING OF HEAVEN · ATHENE · GODDESS OF WISDOM · HERMES · THE MESSENGER · ARTEMIS · ... OF HUNTING · APHR...

CLASSICAL GREECE

In Greek mythology there were Four Ages of Man: the Golden, Silver, Bronze, and Iron (or Heroic) Ages

THE GOLDEN AGE

The Golden Age was said to be the best of times, when everyone was happy. In Greek history Athens had a Golden Age in the fifth century B.C.

BUT...

What does it say?

DORIANS GO HOME!

Before the Golden Age there was a Dark Age, illiterate Dorians inv... the Greek mainland

After 900 B.C. life improved for a while until the PERSIAN WARS began in 499 B.C.

The Dark Ages lasted from 1100 B.C. to 900 B.C.

Greek trade revived

776 B.C. Olympic Games were held

Olympus

PERSIAN DOGS!

GREEK SCUM!

THE GOLDEN AGE OF ATHENS 460-431 B.C.

This Golden Age was also called the AGE OF PERICLES. He was the leading statesman in Athens. He helped

PERICLES

plan the city, and encouraged its art and literature.

The GOLDEN AGE

A time of great achievement for Athens and its people

THEATER

WHAT DID HE SAY?

HMMPH. IT'S ALL GREEK TO ME.

The poet Sophocles wrote plays for the Athenian theater. All the actors had to be men, and they wore special masks.

THE PERSIAN WARS c.499-479 B.C.

In 490 B.C. the Greek city-states united against the Persian invaders and won at Marathon. Ten years later, the Persians returned and won at Thermopylae. But the Greeks won, finally, in 476 B.C.

Thermopylae · Marathon · Athens · Salamis

News of a Greek victory at Marathon in 490 B.C. was taken 26 miles to Athens by a runner. This is the origin of our modern athletic MARATHON.

...after defeating the Persians at Salamis and

THE PARTHENON

This temple to Athene was begun in 447 B.C. on the Acropolis, the hill above Athens.

ARISTOTLE

Socrates, Plato, and his pupil Aristotle were great Athenian philosophers. Aristotle is called the father of modern scientific thought; he was also Alexander's tutor.

THINKS

SOCRATES · PLATO

Male citizens could vote on important city issues.

POLITIC...

The physician Hippocrates' oath to care for his patients is still sworn by doctors today.

!◦

THE HIPPOCRATIC OATH

The spe... podiu... at th... Pnyx

ALEXANDER

The Golden Age in Athens was cut short by war with Sparta, but there was another Greek Golden Age under Alexander the Great.

Alexander conquered Egypt.

Between 334 and 326 B.C., Alexander built up a huge empire, which included both Egypt and Persia. He reached India, but he died young aged only 33, in 323 B.C. His empire did not last long.

16

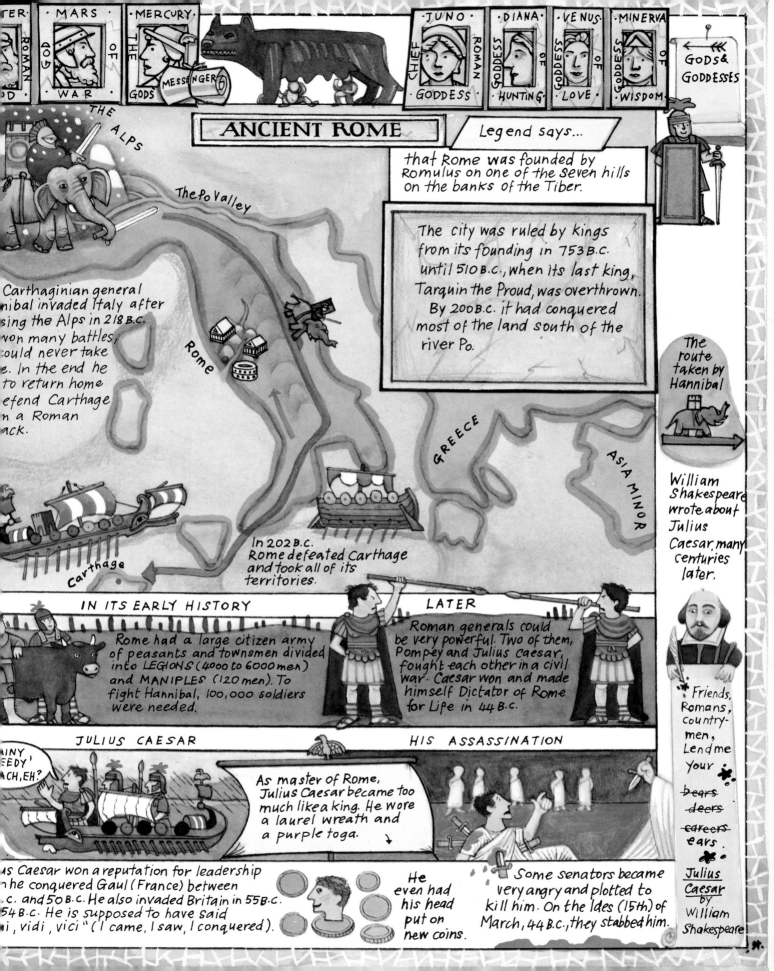

MARS ROMAN GOD OF WAR

MERCURY THE MESSENGER OF THE GODS

JUNO CHIEF ROMAN GODDESS

DIANA ROMAN GODDESS OF HUNTING

VENUS GODDESS OF LOVE

MINERVA GODDESS OF WISDOM

GODS & GODDESSES

ANCIENT ROME

THE ALPS

The Po Valley

Legend says...

that Rome was founded by Romulus on one of the seven hills on the banks of the Tiber.

The city was ruled by kings from its founding in 753 B.C. until 510 B.C., when its last king, Tarquin the Proud, was overthrown. By 200 B.C. it had conquered most of the land south of the river Po.

Carthaginian general [Han]nibal invaded Italy after [cros]sing the Alps in 218 B.C. [He] won many battles, [but] could never take [Rome]. In the end he [had] to return home [to d]efend Carthage [from] a Roman [att]ack.

Rome

GREECE

ASIA MINOR

Carthage

In 202 B.C. Rome defeated Carthage and took all of its territories.

The route taken by Hannibal

William Shakespeare wrote about Julius Caesar, many centuries later.

IN ITS EARLY HISTORY

Rome had a large citizen army of peasants and townsmen divided into LEGIONS (4000 to 6000 men) and MANIPLES (120 men). To fight Hannibal, 100,000 soldiers were needed.

LATER

Roman generals could be very powerful. Two of them, Pompey and Julius Caesar, fought each other in a civil war. Caesar won and made himself Dictator of Rome for Life in 44 B.C.

JULIUS CAESAR

'[M]INY [GR]EEDY [PE]ACH, EH?'

As master of Rome, Julius Caesar became too much like a king. He wore a laurel wreath and a purple toga.

HIS ASSASSINATION

[Juli]us Caesar won a reputation for leadership [whe]n he conquered Gaul (France) between [5. B].C. and 50 B.C. He also invaded Britain in 55 B.C. [and] 54 B.C. He is supposed to have said ["ven]i, vidi, vici" (I came, I saw, I conquered).

He even had his head put on new coins.

Some senators became very angry and plotted to kill him. On the Ides (15th) of March, 44 B.C., they stabbed him.

Friends, Romans, country-men, Lend me your
~~bears~~
~~deers~~
~~careers~~
ears.

Julius Caesar by William Shakespeare

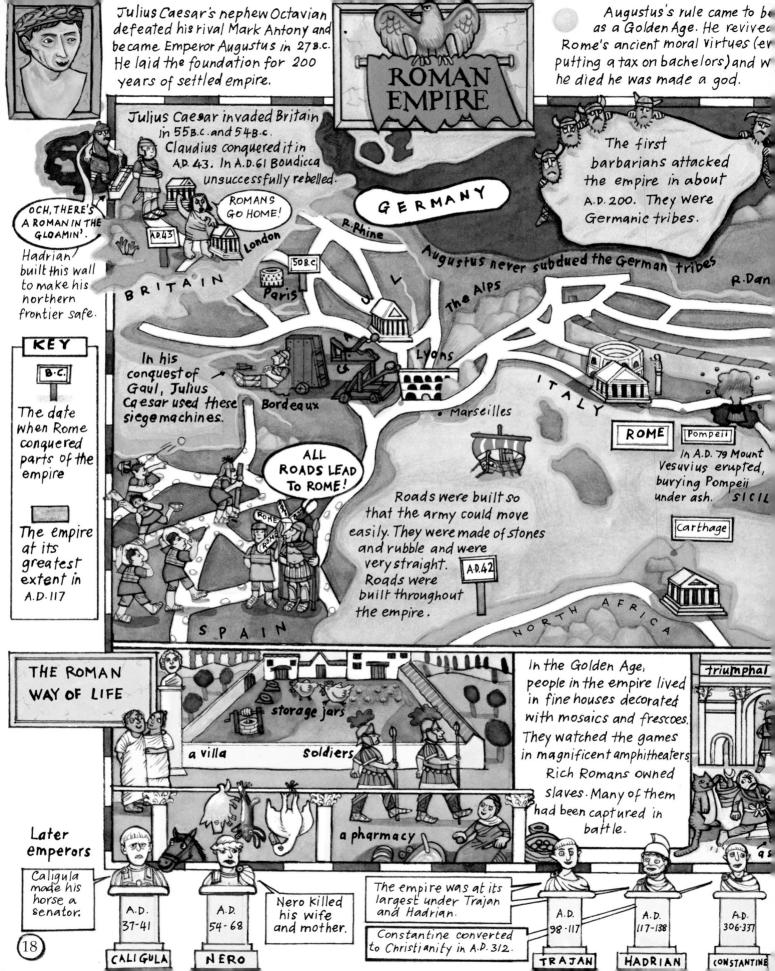

Julius Caesar's nephew Octavian defeated his rival Mark Antony and became Emperor Augustus in 27 B.C. He laid the foundation for 200 years of settled empire.

ROMAN EMPIRE

Augustus's rule came to be as a Golden Age. He revive Rome's ancient moral virtues (e putting a tax on bachelors) and w he died he was made a god.

Julius Caesar invaded Britain in 55 B.C. and 54 B.C. Claudius conquered it in A.D. 43. In A.D. 61 Boudicca unsuccessfully rebelled.

ROMANS GO HOME!

A.D. 43

OCH, THERE'S A ROMAN IN THE GLOAMIN'.

Hadrian built this wall to make his northern frontier safe.

The first barbarians attacked the empire in about A.D. 200. They were Germanic tribes.

GERMANY

R. Rhine

Augustus never subdued the German tribes

R. Dan

London

50 B.C.

Paris

BRITAIN

The Alps

Lyons

ITALY

KEY

B.C.

The date when Rome conquered parts of the empire

The empire at its greatest extent in A.D. 117

In his conquest of Gaul, Julius Caesar used these siege machines.

Bordeaux

• Marseilles

ALL ROADS LEAD TO ROME!

ROME   Pompeii

In A.D. 79 Mount Vesuvius erupted, burying Pompeii under ash. SICIL

Carthage

Roads were built so that the army could move easily. They were made of stones and rubble and were very straight. Roads were built throughout the empire.

A.D. 42

SPAIN

NORTH AFRICA

THE ROMAN WAY OF LIFE

storage jars

a villa   soldiers

a pharmacy

In the Golden Age, people in the empire lived in fine houses decorated with mosaics and frescoes. They watched the games in magnificent amphitheaters. Rich Romans owned slaves. Many of them had been captured in battle.

triumphal

Later emperors

Caligula made his horse a senator.

A.D. 37-41

CALIGULA

A.D. 54-68

NERO

Nero killed his wife and mother.

The empire was at its largest under Trajan and Hadrian.

Constantine converted to Christianity in A.D. 312.

A.D. 98-117

TRAJAN

A.D. 117-138

HADRIAN

A.D. 306-337

CONSTANTINE

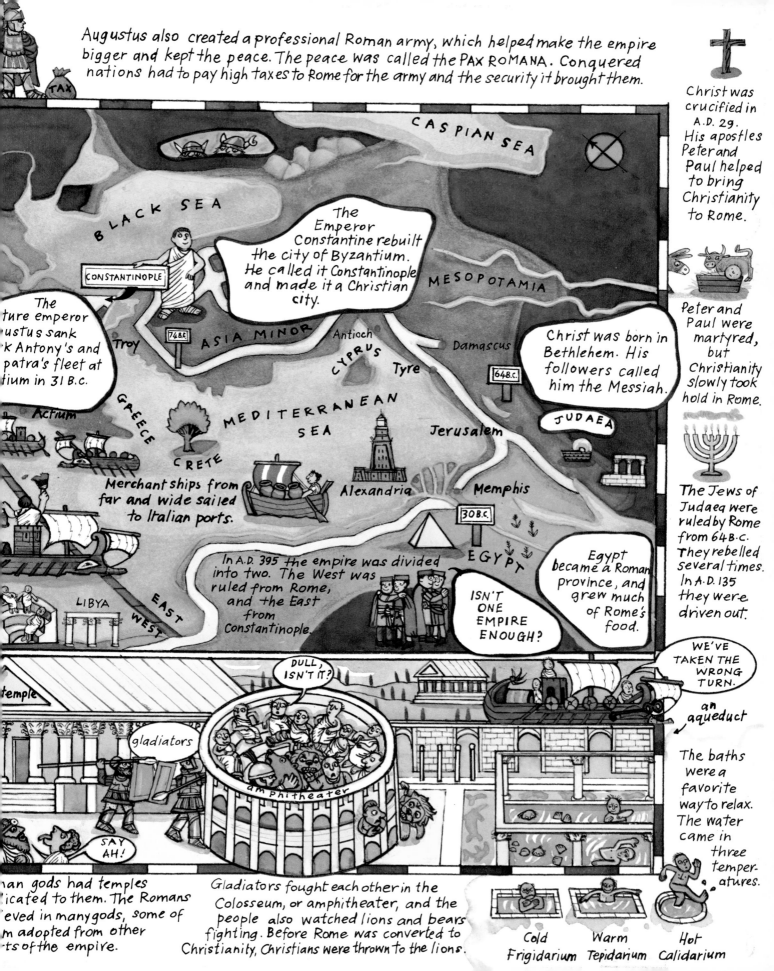

Augustus also created a professional Roman army, which helped make the empire bigger and kept the peace. The peace was called the PAX ROMANA. Conquered nations had to pay high taxes to Rome for the army and the security it brought them.

TAX

CASPIAN SEA

BLACK SEA

CONSTANTINOPLE

The Emperor Constantine rebuilt the city of Byzantium. He called it Constantinople and made it a Christian city.

74 B.C.

MESOPOTAMIA

ASIA MINOR

Antioch

Troy

Damascus

64 B.C.

CYPRUS

Tyre

The future emperor Augustus sank Mark Antony's and Cleopatra's fleet at Actium in 31 B.C.

GREECE

Actium

MEDITERRANEAN SEA

CRETE

Christ was born in Bethlehem. His followers called him the Messiah.

JUDAEA

Jerusalem

Merchant ships from far and wide sailed to Italian ports.

Alexandria

Memphis

30 B.C.

In A.D. 395 the empire was divided into two. The West was ruled from Rome, and the East from Constantinople.

EGYPT

Egypt became a Roman province, and grew much of Rome's food.

ISN'T ONE EMPIRE ENOUGH?

LIBYA

EAST

WEST

Christ was crucified in A.D. 29. His apostles Peter and Paul helped to bring Christianity to Rome.

Peter and Paul were martyred, but Christianity slowly took hold in Rome.

The Jews of Judaea were ruled by Rome from 64 B.C. They rebelled several times. In A.D. 135 they were driven out.

WE'VE TAKEN THE WRONG TURN.

an aqueduct

DULL, ISN'T IT?

temple

gladiators

amphitheater

SAY AH!

...an gods had temples ...icated to them. The Romans ...eved in many gods, some of ...m adopted from other ...ts of the empire.

Gladiators fought each other in the Colosseum, or amphitheater, and the people also watched lions and bears fighting. Before Rome was converted to Christianity, Christians were thrown to the lions.

The baths were a favorite way to relax. The water came in three temperatures.

Cold Frigidarium

Warm Tepidarium

Hot Calidarium

Dark Ages in Europe
The Barbarian Invasions

When Rome fell, the Western Empire moved into the European Middle Ages. These began with **THE DARK AGES**.

Barbarians drove the Britons west and divided the country into new Anglo-Saxon and Jutish kingdoms.

Legend says that the British King Arthur tried to stop the Anglo-Saxon advance.

In the eighth and ninth centuries Vikings invaded Ireland and N. England.

449 After the Romans had left, Angles and Saxons invaded England.

As the Roman Empire grew weak, Germanic tribes and the Huns attacked. Rome and the Western Empire were conquered, and so in the East Constantinople became the power.

Baltic Sea

GOTHS

YOU GOTHIC HORROR!

ANGLES

SAXONS

London

In the fifth and sixth centuries the Franks were successful here.

Paris

FRANKS

SUEVI

ALEMANNI

BURGUNDIANS

HUNS

451 Attila in Gaul

452 Attila in north Italy

HUN

OSTRO

VISIGOTHS

Ravenna

493 Ostrogoths ruled all of Italy.

Rome

732 Charles Martel stopped the N. Africans at Poitiers.

Roman soldiers and their commander (whom they had elected emperor) abandoned England and crossed to Gaul.

405 Vandals overran Gaul.

416 Visigoths ruled Toulouse and parts of Aquitaine.

In 410 ROME was attacked by Alaric and the Goths; Ravenna became the capital. In 455 the Vandal Gaiseric attacked. Rome and the West fell in 476.

Carthage

ARABS and NORTH AFRICANS

SUEVI

VANDALS

VISIGOTHS

411-585 The Suevi ruled here.

409 Vandals overran Spain.

416 Visigoths conquered Vandal Spain.

In the 470s the Vandals built a fleet of ships. Led by Gaiseric, they took over some Mediterranean islands.

429 Vandals set up a kingdom in North Africa. They threatened the corn supply to Rome.

ARABS & NORTH AFRICANS

VANDALS

WHERE'S THE SOCCER GAME?

VANDALS

Muslims from the north of Africa invaded Spain in 711.

Continuing the advance of Islam, Muslims defeated the Visigoths. By 718 they had conquered most of Spain.

In the centuries after A.D. 400, when Europe was living through its Dark Ages, many civilizations flourished in the rest of the World.

EUROPE? NEVER HEARD OF IT.

EUROPE? WHERE'S THAT?

The Islamic empire before 850

Persia's Sassanian empire

ASIA

ANYONE AT HOME?

INUIT (Eskimo)

The KORAN

Muhammad died in 632, and a learned Islamic civilization grew up as his followers conquered nearby lands like north India and Persia. They carried those cultural traditions and learning through the Middle East.

OH, GIVE ME A HOME WHERE THE BUFFALO ROAM.

The Americas were isolated from the rest of the world, and writing appeared later here than in Asia or Europe. However, there were large cities and highly skilled craftwork.

PLAINS TRIBES

corn

PUEBLO DWELLERS

North America

In North America native Americans hunted and farmed.

carpet weaving

$$118 + 19 + 37 = 174$$

mathematics

astronomy

medicine

architecture

The Dome the Roc

Europe

Isl

Teotihuacán

OLMECS

Chichén Itzá

MAYANS

Central America

By the fourth century the OLMECS had invented hieroglyphic writing and an astronomical calendar. Their successors built Teotihuacán, the first American city. It was a religious center with stone pyramids and other public buildings.

Pyramid

pottery figure

ceramics

Africa

GHANA

GOLD

South America

Central America was the first area to develop.

MOCHICA people

THE RAIN FOREST

The Kingdom of Ghana in the eighth century was called the "Land of Gold." It became rich from the trade between Africans and Arabs. The Arabs exchanged copper, weapons, tools, and horses for African gold, ivory, slaves, and animal skins.

The Mayans were clever astronomers.

At this time, the MAYANS lived in the tropical rain forests of Mexico and Central America. In their ceremonial centers they built temples, pyramids and courts. By watching the stars carefully, they invented a calendar, and they worshipped according to it.

Lake Titicaca Tiahuanaco City

TIAHUANACO CULTURE

Between 200 and 600 the MOCHICA built pyramids, like their neighbors to the north. To the south, a little later, the city of Tiahuanaco became a religious center.

Foreigners mostly stayed away from the African Interior because of diseas

On the other hand, they never managed to invent the keystone arch or the wheel.

Easter Island

Kon-Tiki, a balsa-wood raft

S. America

In about 400, Easter Island in the Pacific was settled and magnificent statues were made there. The settlers may have been Polynesians from the west, but some people think they came from South America.

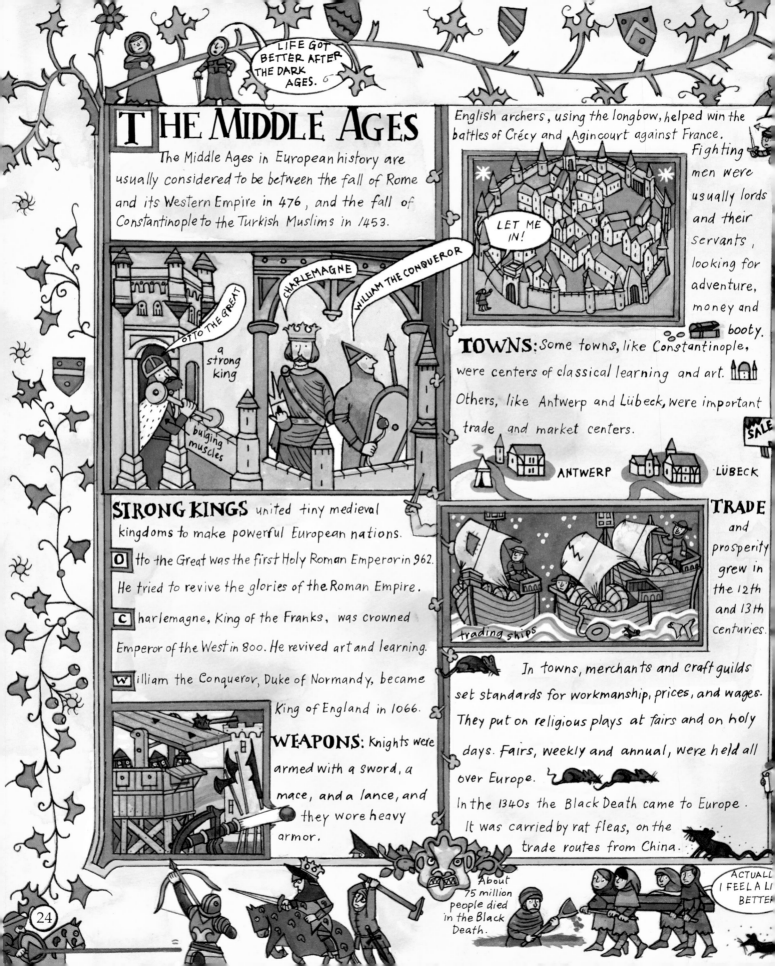

THE MIDDLE AGES

The Middle Ages in European history are usually considered to be between the fall of Rome and its Western Empire in 476, and the fall of Constantinople to the Turkish Muslims in 1453.

LIFE GOT BETTER AFTER THE DARK AGES.

OTTO THE GREAT — a strong king — bulging muscles

CHARLEMAGNE

WILLIAM THE CONQUEROR

STRONG KINGS united tiny medieval kingdoms to make powerful European nations.

Otto the Great was the first Holy Roman Emperor in 962. He tried to revive the glories of the Roman Empire.

Charlemagne, King of the Franks, was crowned Emperor of the West in 800. He revived art and learning.

William the Conqueror, Duke of Normandy, became King of England in 1066.

WEAPONS: Knights were armed with a sword, a mace, and a lance, and they wore heavy armor.

English archers, using the longbow, helped win the battles of Crécy and Agincourt against France.

LET ME IN!

Fighting men were usually lords and their servants, looking for adventure, money and booty.

TOWNS: Some towns, like Constantinople, were centers of classical learning and art. Others, like Antwerp and Lübeck, were important trade and market centers.

SALE

ANTWERP   LÜBECK

TRADE and prosperity grew in the 12th and 13th centuries.

trading ships

In towns, merchants and craft guilds set standards for workmanship, prices, and wages. They put on religious plays at fairs and on holy days. Fairs, weekly and annual, were held all over Europe.

In the 1340s the Black Death came to Europe. It was carried by rat fleas, on the trade routes from China.

About 75 million people died in the Black Death.

ACTUALLY I FEEL A LI[TTLE] BETTER

Crusaders left Europe and fought to take the Holy Land from the Muslims.

swish

Finally the Crusaders lost Jerusalem in 1187.

The feudal system was not always strictly organized.

THE CHURCH and

monasteries became powerful and wealthy landowners in the Middle Ages. The best masons in Europe helped to build the great cathedrals. Pilgrims traveled all over Europe to see the "relics" of saints placed in these cathedrals. Some pilgrims also visited the Holy Land.

The Holy Land

Monasteries became centers of learning. Some monks were artists and illuminators, and others tended the sick in the infirmaries.

THE FEUDAL SYSTEM

← open-field farming →

This system was a way of organizing society. In general, powerful people granted men land in return for duties. These duties might include military service, or just paying rents and dues.

The Normans made the system stronger in England when they conquered the country in 1066.

MYTHS

Many people believed in monsters like dragons and chimeras, and the gaping jaws of Hell; and they thought that there were men in Africa whose head grew beneath their shoulders. People also believed in witches and wizards who could cast magic spells.

Monsters

PUNISHMENT:

The courts of the Inquisition tortured heretics (those who disagreed with the Church) and sometimes burned them at the stake.

WHERE ARE THEY?

Other forms of punishment

THAT TRICK'S OLD HAT.

SH IT!

THE CAT LOOKS FAMILIAR.

ducking

Wrongdoers could be executed by the sword, ax, or rope. Minor offenders were put in the stocks or pillory.

sword   ax   rope   stocks and pillory

Christian orders of knights on the first Crusade took Jerusalem from the Turks in 1099. They held it only until 1187.

A Medieval Town

I WILL CONQUER THE WORLD!

Trade

English wool was sent to the Continent.

Towns held regular trade fairs and markets.

Hanseatic League merchants traded between northern and Baltic ports.

The Chinese sent silks, jewels, and spices to Europe along the Silk Road.

Muslim Turks stopped Christians from visiting shrines in the Holy Land. This sparked off the Christian Crusades.

THE HOLY LAND

Medieval trade was easiest by water.

a trading ship

Nomadic Mongols swept through Asia in the 13th century. Genghis Khan and his successors conquered large parts of the Middle East, China, India, Russia, and Persia.

ASIA

In the town t were members many differ guilds.

entertain

armorer

barber

tailor

butcher

I CAN'T BEAR IT. IT'S A GRIZZLY LIFE.

merchants

baker

a mystery play

OINK!

dyer

Pilgrims visited holy places in their own country and abroad.

carter

Sweyn Forkbeard · Eric the Red · Charles the Bald · Geoffrey the Handsome · Harold Harefoot · Ethelred the Unready · Henry the Black · Pedro the

Medieval rulers

26

MICHELANGELO Buonarroti (1475-1564) was a sculptor, painter, architect, and poet. He painted the ceiling of the Vatican's Sistine Chapel in Rome.

Michelangelo and Leonardo da Vinci are known as RENAISSANCE MEN.

This means that they were well educated and clever at many different activities.

HOW SICKENINGLY CLEVER.

Leonardo DA VINCI (1452-1519) was a painter, sculptor, architect, engineer, musician, and inventor.

The RENAISSANCE
The rebirth of classical ideas in the 14th through 16th centuries

The Church in medieval times was the main educator of the people. But it was tied to the past and did not like new ideas.

In Italy in the 14th and 15th centuries there was a move away from Church teaching. Instead, scholars became interested in the classical philosophers, writers, and sculptors of ancient Greece and Rome. These men inspired talented people in Italy to experiment and make progress in many areas of study.

This rebirth, or "Renaissance," of ideas spread around Europe.

St. Peter's, ROME

Michelangelo helped design St. Peter's in Ro

Michelang

He co Brunelleschi's dome in Floren

Leonardo's design for manned flight

Renaissance artists used perspective and the effects of light to make their paintings appear more three-dimensional.

OH, IT'S LISA. SHE'S A REAL MOANER.

SMILE!

For the first time real models sat for paintings.

Mona Lisa

The study of anatomy helped painters represent the human body.

Leonardo's flying machine

Leonardo's inventions

water floats

an armored car

an exploding shell

Another well-rounded Renaissa man was King Henry VIII of England. He was a sportsman, musician, and linguist. He is a well known for having married six times.

Henry VII

(28)

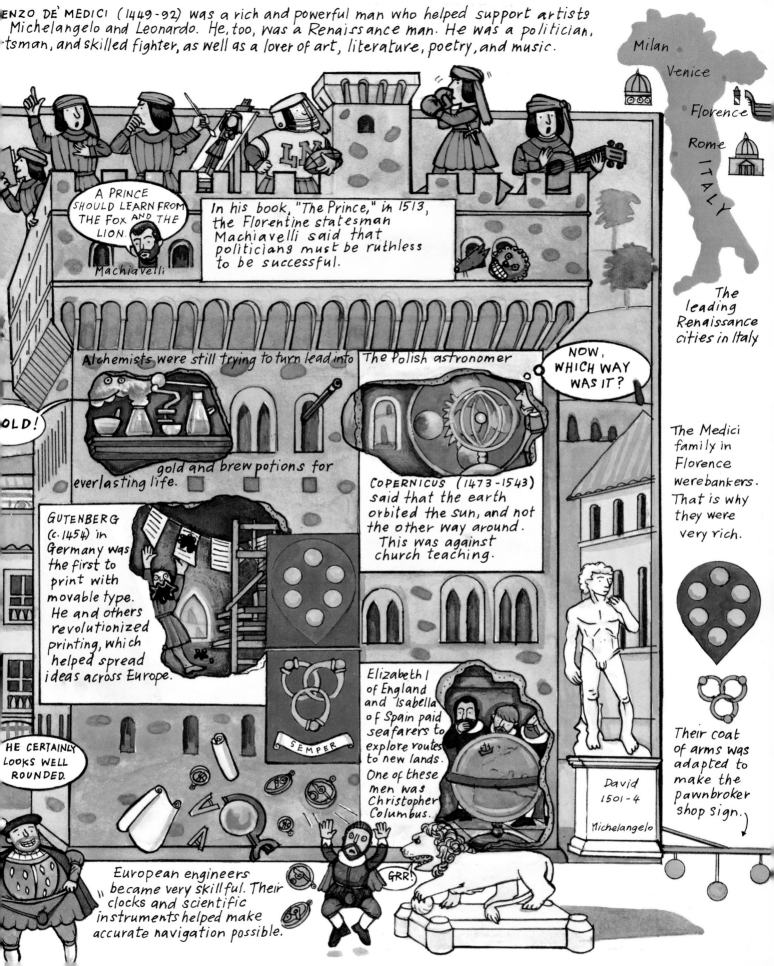

EUROPEAN EXPLORATION

Around 1500, China and the Ottoman Empire were very important powers. Then, after 1500, so[me] European countries sent seafarers around the globe. Europe began to dominate the wor[ld] and change the course of history.

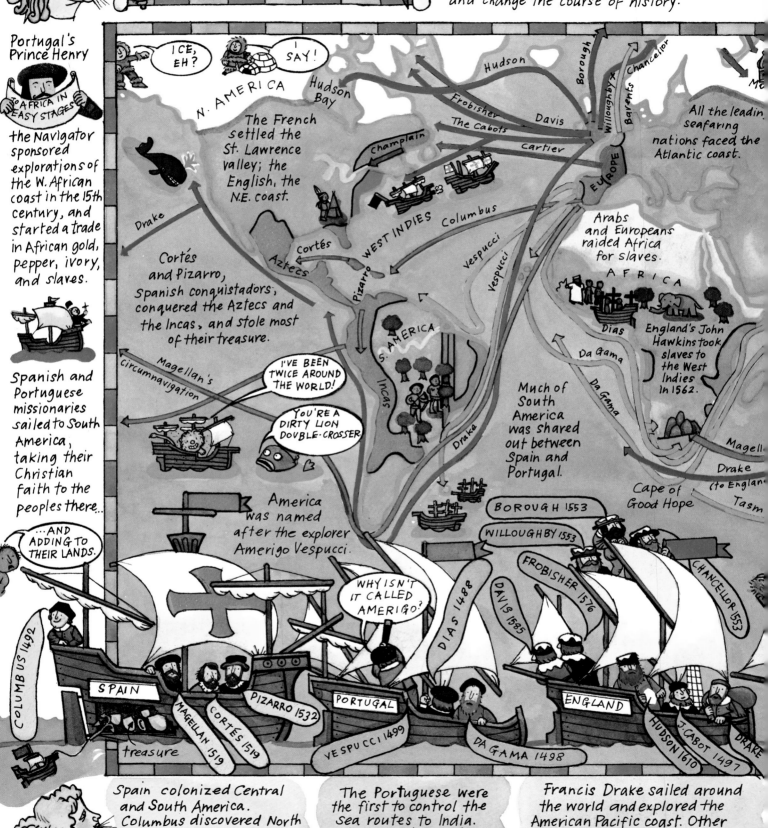

Portugal's Prince Henry the Navigator sponsored explorations of the W. African coast in the 15th century, and started a trade in African gold, pepper, ivory, and slaves.

Spanish and Portuguese missionaries sailed to South America, taking their Christian faith to the peoples there...

...AND ADDING TO THEIR LANDS.

The French settled the St. Lawrence valley; the English, the N.E. coast.

Cortés and Pizarro, Spanish conquistadors, conquered the Aztecs and the Incas, and stole most of their treasure.

I'VE BEEN TWICE AROUND THE WORLD!

YOU'RE A DIRTY LION DOUBLE-CROSSER!

America was named after the explorer Amerigo Vespucci.

WHY ISN'T IT CALLED AMERIGO?

ICE, EH?

I SAY!

All the leading seafaring nations faced the Atlantic coast.

Arabs and Europeans raided Africa for slaves.

England's John Hawkins took slaves to the West Indies in 1562.

Much of South America was shared out between Spain and Portugal.

Cape of Good Hope

Magellan's circumnavigation

BOROUGH 1553
WILLOUGHBY 1553
FROBISHER 1576
CHANCELLOR 1553
DIAS 1488
DAVIS 1585
COLUMBUS 1492
MAGELLAN 1519
CORTES 1519
PIZARRO 1532
VESPUCCI 1499
DA GAMA 1498
HUDSON 1610
J. CABOT 1497

SPAIN

PORTUGAL

ENGLAND

treasure

Spain colonized Central and South America. Columbus discovered North America, and Magellan led the first expedition to sail around the world.

The Portuguese were the first to control the sea routes to India. They settled in China, Africa and Brazil.

Francis Drake sailed around the world and explored the American Pacific coast. Other English explorers sailed the northern oceans to America and Russia.

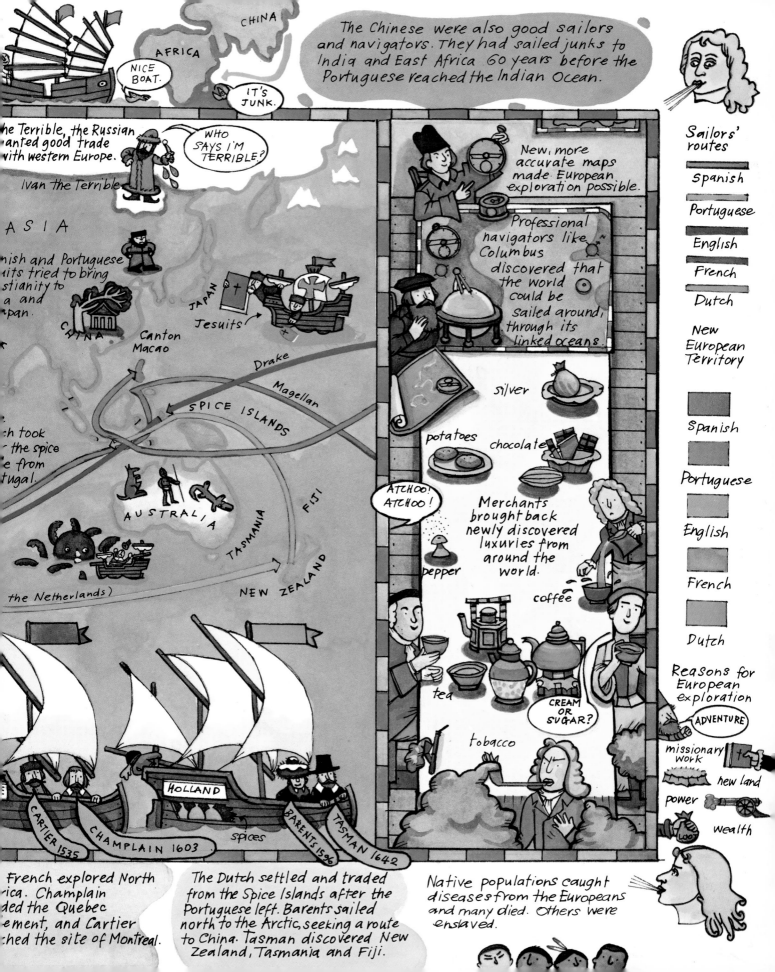

People were pardoned for their sins, if they paid the Church for indulgences. This annoyed a monk called Martin Luther.

Luther wrote the 95 Theses, criticizing the Catholic Church,

and nailed them to the door of Wittenberg Palace church.

Elizabeth I of England was Henry VIII's daughter. Her navy destroyed Philip of Spain's fleet, the Armada.

The REFORMATION & COUNTER-REFORMATION

CHURCH LEADERS HAVE LOST TOUCH WITH THE FAITHFUL.

ERASMUS was a Catholic whose reforming ideas influenced 16th-century Europe.

The Church of the Protestant Reformation

LUTHER CALVIN ZWINGLI KNOX HENRY VIII

In the early 16th century, some people began to question Catholic Church teaching. They wanted simpler worship and more Bible teaching.
Other people thought that Church leaders were corrupt, and so refused to accept their authority.
Martin Luther protested in 1517, and began the Reformation Movement.

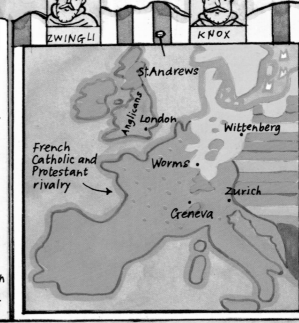

| Lutherans |
| Zwinglians and Calvinists |
| Roman Catholics |
| Catholic and Protestant mixed |
| The Muslim Ottoman Empire |

Bibles were first prin and put into people's languages in the 16th century.

Calvin, the French theologian, wanted Geneva (where he lived in Switzerland) to be ruled by strict Protestant rules.

The inside of a Calvinist church was often plain and simple.

Zwingli led Switzerland's Protestant movement for a while.

Scotland's John Knox criticized the Pope in his sermons. Some of Knox's followers pulled down the cathedral at St. Andrews.

HOW TO DISSOLVE MONASTERIES

Printing presses helped spread Luther ideas i Germa and elsewhe

England's Henry VIII wa called "Defender of the F for opposing Luther. he argued with the P over a divorce, and thou he remained a Catholic, h made himself head of the English Church and dissolved its monasterie

SO THERE'S NOWHERE TO HIDE!

In 1558 the Catholic Queen Mary I of England died, and her Protestant half sister Elizabeth, came to the throne. She established Protestant worship in 1563, but both Catholics and Puritans dissented from the Church of England. Those discovered plotting against her were executed.

Elizabeth I Queen of England

Magnificent country houses were built in Elizabeth's reign

LONGLEAT

Elizabeth was very clever. As a young princess she read widely, and learned to speak Latin, Greek, French, and Italian.

Elizabeth I reigned for 44 years. She was a popular and clever ruler, and had many brilliant courtiers. Her seafarers sailed the world, and Shakespeare was writing plays. It was an exciting age, but at the end of Elizabeth's reign England was suffering from crippling debts.

CITY OF LONDON

Royal Exchange

Merchants formed companies which traded overseas.

Mary, Queen of Scots, was beheaded for treason in 1587.

The Cath Mary, of S

a cockpit

In Elizabethan times people were hanged for witchcraft, and there was begging in the streets.

Ye Olde London

A law in 1601 did help provide work and shelter for the poor.

England's navy beat the Spanish Armada in 1588.

To the Armada ▶

The Globe

ALL THE WORLD'S A STAGE.

OH, LOOK! SHAKESPEARE'S BOTTOM.

YUK. THAT'S THE PITS.

William Byrd was the first important English writer of madrigals.

Nicholas Hilliard was a skillful painter of small portraits. He was well known throughout Europe.

Ye Elizabethan Court

From 1558 to 1598 Lord Burghley faithfully advised the queen.

Raleigh tried but failed to establish a Virgini Colony. He did bring tobacc and potatoes to England.

Leicester Essex Lord Burghley Sir Francis Drake Sir Walter Raleigh John Whi Archbisho Canterb

Elizabeth did not marry and have heirs. She was called the "Virgin Queen."

The Earls of Leicester and Essex were favorites of the queen.

Drake sailed around the world from 1577 to 1580 and raided Spanish America.

England former Catholi became Protestant i Elizabeth's rei

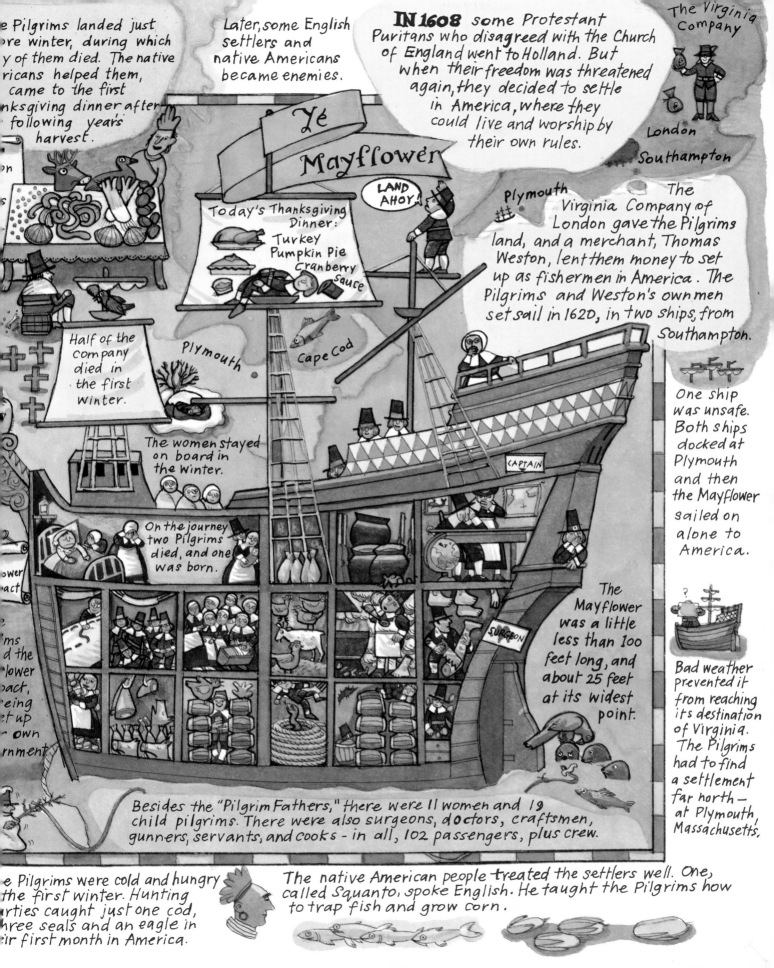

...e Pilgrims landed just ...re winter, during which ...y of them died. The native ...ricans helped them, ...came to the first ...nksgiving dinner after ...following years' harvest.

Later, some English settlers and native Americans became enemies.

IN 1608 some Protestant Puritans who disagreed with the Church of England went to Holland. But when their freedom was threatened again, they decided to settle in America, where they could live and worship by their own rules.

The Virginia Company

The Virginia Company of London gave the Pilgrims land, and a merchant, Thomas Weston, lent them money to set up as fishermen in America. The Pilgrims and Weston's own men set sail in 1620, in two ships, from Southampton.

London
Southampton
Plymouth

Ye Mayflower

LAND AHOY!

Today's Thanksgiving Dinner:
Turkey
Pumpkin Pie
Cranberry sauce

Cape Cod

Plymouth

Half of the company died in the first winter.

The women stayed on board in the winter.

On the journey two Pilgrims died, and one was born.

CAPTAIN

SURGEON

One ship was unsafe. Both ships docked at Plymouth and then the Mayflower sailed on alone to America.

The Mayflower was a little less than 100 feet long, and about 25 feet at its widest point.

Bad weather prevented it from reaching its destination of Virginia. The Pilgrims had to find a settlement far north — at Plymouth, Massachusetts,

Besides the "Pilgrim Fathers," there were 11 women and 19 child pilgrims. There were also surgeons, doctors, craftsmen, gunners, servants, and cooks - in all, 102 passengers, plus crew.

...e Pilgrims were cold and hungry ...the first winter. Hunting ...rties caught just one cod, ...hree seals and an eagle in ...ir first month in America.

The native American people treated the settlers well. One, called Squanto, spoke English. He taught the Pilgrims how to trap fish and grow corn.

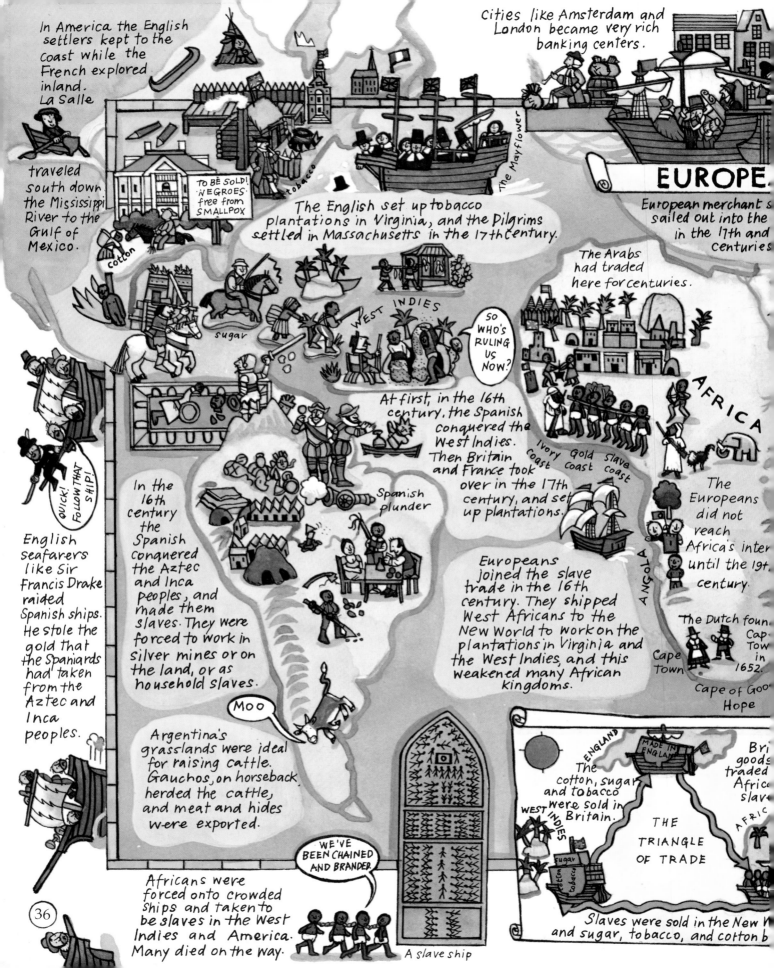

In America the English settlers kept to the coast while the French explored inland. La Salle traveled south down the Mississippi River to the Gulf of Mexico.

TO BE SOLD! NEGROES free from SMALLPOX

cotton

tobacco

The Mayflower

The English set up tobacco plantations in Virginia, and the Pilgrims settled in Massachusetts in the 17th century.

Cities like Amsterdam and London became very rich banking centers.

EUROPE

European merchant s sailed out into the in the 17th and centuries

The Arabs had traded here for centuries.

AFRICA

sugar

WEST INDIES

SO WHO'S RULING US NOW?

At first, in the 16th century, the Spanish conquered the West Indies. Then Britain and France took over in the 17th century, and set up plantations.

Ivory Coast Gold coast Slave coast

The Europeans did not reach Africa's inter until the 19t century.

English seafarers like Sir Francis Drake raided Spanish ships. He stole the gold that the Spaniards had taken from the Aztec and Inca peoples.

QUICK! FOLLOW THAT SHIP!

In the 16th century the Spanish conquered the Aztec and Inca peoples, and made them slaves. They were forced to work in silver mines or on the land, or as household slaves.

Spanish plunder

Europeans joined the slave trade in the 16th century. They shipped West Africans to the New World to work on the plantations in Virginia and the West Indies, and this weakened many African kingdoms.

ANGOLA

Cape Town

The Dutch foun. Cap Tow in 1652.

Cape of Goo Hope

Moo

Argentina's grasslands were ideal for raising cattle. Gauchos, on horseback, herded the cattle, and meat and hides were exported.

WE'VE BEEN CHAINED AND BRANDED.

ENGLAND

MADE IN ENGLAND

The cotton, sugar and tobacco were sold in Britain.

WEST INDIES

sugar cotton tobacco

THE TRIANGLE OF TRADE

Bri goods traded Afric slav

AFRIC

36

Africans were forced onto crowded ships and taken to be slaves in the West Indies and America. Many died on the way.

A slave ship

Slaves were sold in the New and sugar, tobacco, and cotton b

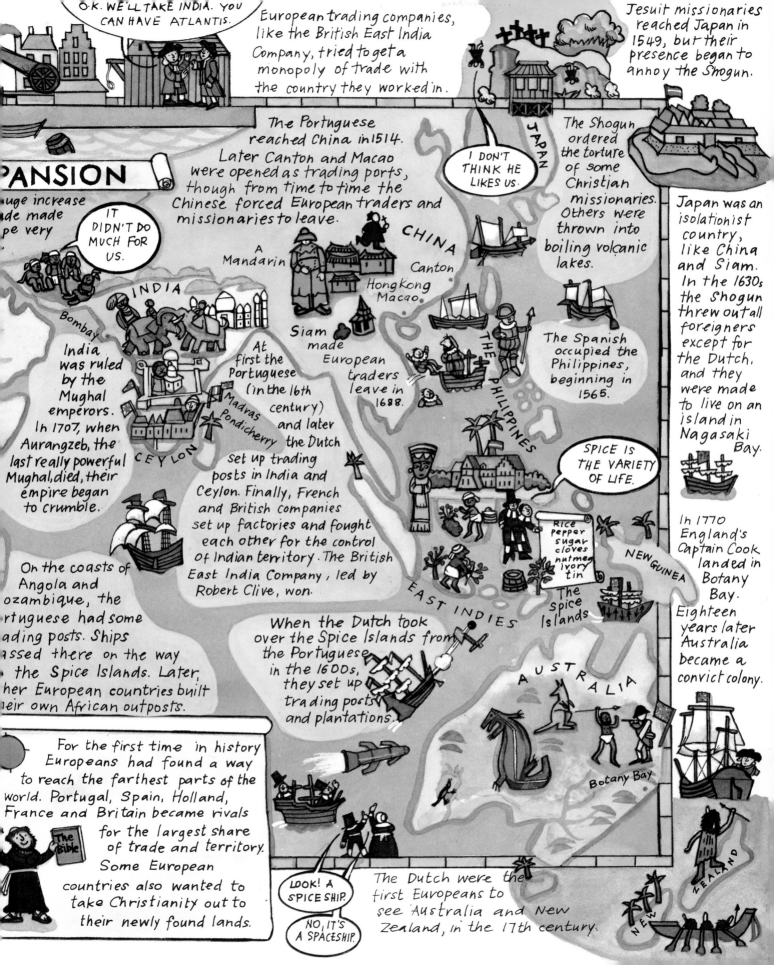

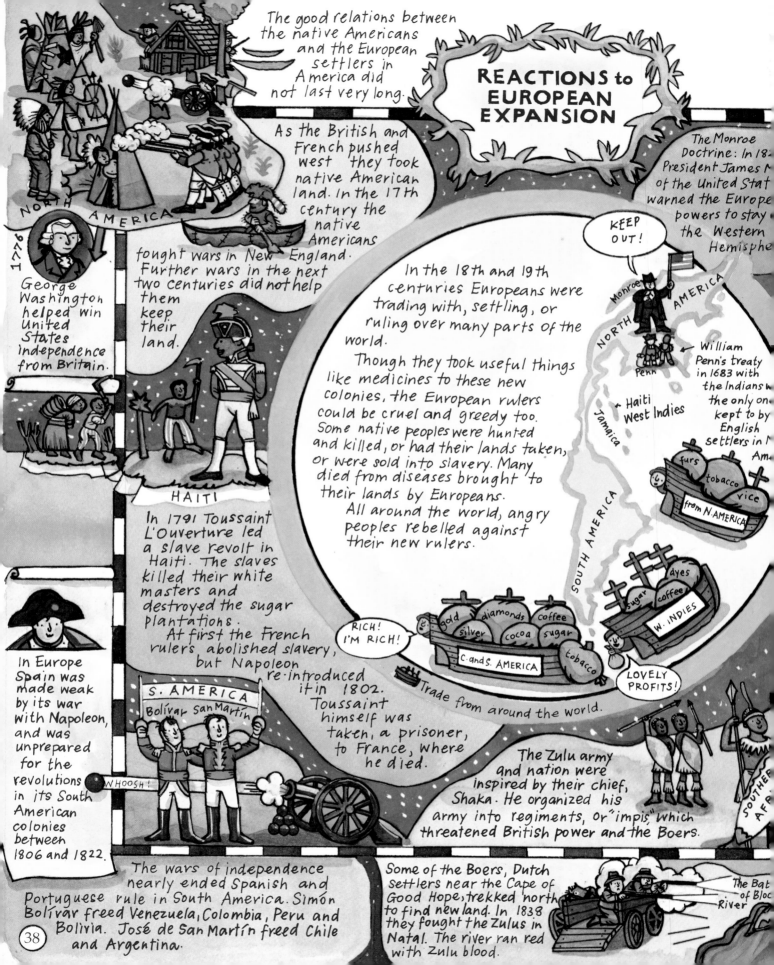

The good relations between the native Americans and the European settlers in America did not last very long.

REACTIONS to EUROPEAN EXPANSION

As the British and French pushed west they took native American land. In the 17th century the native Americans fought wars in New England. Further wars in the next two centuries did not help them keep their land.

NORTH AMERICA

1776

George Washington helped win United States independence from Britain.

HAITI

In 1791 Toussaint L'Ouverture led a slave revolt in Haiti. The slaves killed their white masters and destroyed the sugar plantations.
At first the French rulers abolished slavery, but Napoleon re-introduced it in 1802. Toussaint himself was taken, a prisoner, to France, where he died.

In Europe Spain was made weak by its war with Napoleon, and was unprepared for the revolutions in its South American colonies between 1806 and 1822.

S. AMERICA
Bolívar San Martín
WHOOSH!

The wars of independence nearly ended Spanish and Portuguese rule in South America. Simón Bolívar freed Venezuela, Colombia, Peru and Bolivia. José de San Martín freed Chile and Argentina.

The Monroe Doctrine: In 18- President James M of the United Stat warned the Europe powers to stay the Western Hemisphe

KEEP OUT!

Monroe

NORTH AMERICA

Penn

William Penn's treaty in 1683 with the Indians w the only on kept to by English settlers in N Am.

Haiti
Jamaica
West Indies

furs
tobacco
rice
from N. AMERICA

In the 18th and 19th centuries Europeans were trading with, settling, or ruling over many parts of the world.
Though they took useful things like medicines to these new colonies, the European rulers could be cruel and greedy too. Some native peoples were hunted and killed, or had their lands taken, or were sold into slavery. Many died from diseases brought to their lands by Europeans.
All around the world, angry peoples rebelled against their new rulers.

SOUTH AMERICA

RICH! I'M RICH!

gold diamonds coffee
silver cocoa sugar
tobacco
C. and S. AMERICA

dyes
sugar coffee
W. INDIES

LOVELY PROFITS!

Trade from around the world.

The Zulu army and nation were inspired by their chief, Shaka. He organized his army into regiments, or "impis," which threatened British power and the Boers.

SOUTHER AFR

Some of the Boers, Dutch settlers near the Cape of Good Hope, trekked north to find new land. In 1838 they fought the Zulus in Natal. The river ran red with Zulu blood.

The Bat of Bloc River

38

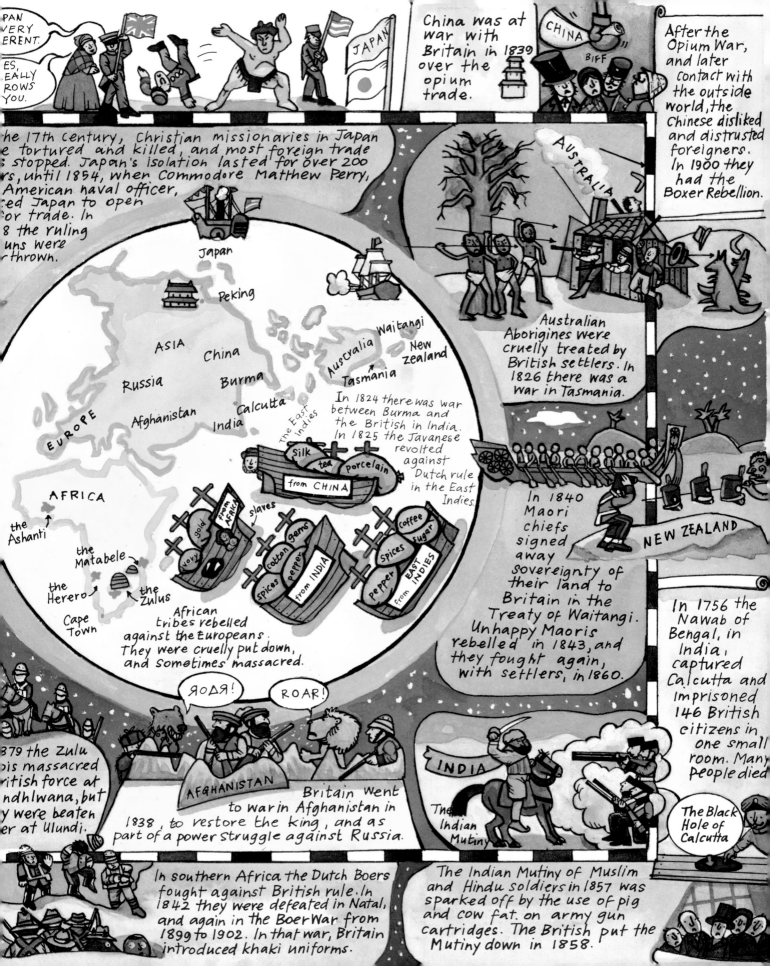

from 1703
Peter made
St. Petersbur[g]
Russia's
capital. It lay closer to the West tha[n]
Moscow, and stayed the capital for
200 years

The splendor of Louis XIV's court was admired at home and by royalty abroad. The palace at Versailles cost $250 million and took 47 years to build.

Versailles

I SUPPOSE I JUST LOST MY HEAD.

L'ETAT, C'EST MOI.

THE AGE OF
KINGS &
QUEENS

FRANCE

RUSSIA

In his
effor[t]

Wester[n]
Russia[n]
court, [he]
put a t[ax]
on bea[rds]
and m[ade]
his nob[les]
cut th[eir]
own bea[rds]
short.

King Charles I of England dissolved Parliament in 1629, and ruled as absolute monarch for 11 years.
After a civil war the Parliamentary side under Oliver Cromwell tried and executed him, in 1649.
This appalled foreign royalty.

GASP!

GASP!

England was now for the first and only time a republic — the Commonwealth — until Charles II was restored in 1660.

THE DEFENESTRATION OF PRAGUE

In the 17th and 18th centuries, much of Europe was ruled by kings and queens whose powers knew very few limits.

These rulers were called ABSOLUTE MONARCHS, and one of the greatest was Louis XIV of France.

Louis XIV

GET UP! WE'RE A STANDING ARMY.

Louis ruled with no parliament, and only courtiers and officials to advise him. Like other absolute monarchs, he had a huge standing army, to

keep the peace at home and to fight rivals and enemies abroad. This led to a century of wars, as the powerful European armies fought one another to show who was strongest.

During their reigns, rulers like Louis spent huge sums of money on their magnificent courts, while more enlightened monarchs used their great power to modernize their countries.

The Sun King
LOUIS XIV (1643–1715).
Louis' reign was a model for all European absolute rulers. He ruled with the help of officials like Cardinal Mazarin, and ordered a huge palace to be built for the court at Versailles.
To pay for it, and his large army (which was almost always at war), Louis taxed his people very heavily. When he died, France was deeply in debt.

WHICH SIDE ARE WE ON?

PETER THE GREAT (1682–1725) had only one year's peace in his 43-year reign. On the whole he was a forward-looking ruler. He tried to modernise and Westernise Russia, bringing in many reforms. He even travelled, disguised, to Holland and Britain, to learn about ships and engineering.

OH N[O]
NO[T]
ANOT[HER]
WA[R]

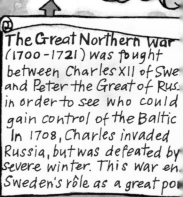

The Great Northern War (1700–1721) was fought between Charles XII of Swe[den] and Peter the Great of Rus[sia], in order to see who could gain control of the Baltic[.] In 1708, Charles invaded Russia, but was defeated by severe winter. This war en[ded] Sweden's rôle as a great po[wer.]

The Thirty Years' War (1618-48) was a complicated war involving many countries. It began wh[en] Bohemian patriots threw two Habsburg councillors from a window in Prague's royal palace[.] At first Protestant countries fought against Catholic Spain and Austria (both ruled by the Habsburgs), but then Catholic France sided with the Protestants. The French succeeded in reducing Habsburg power, and the war ended with the Peace of Westphalia. But many German cities were ruined; hundreds of thousands died.

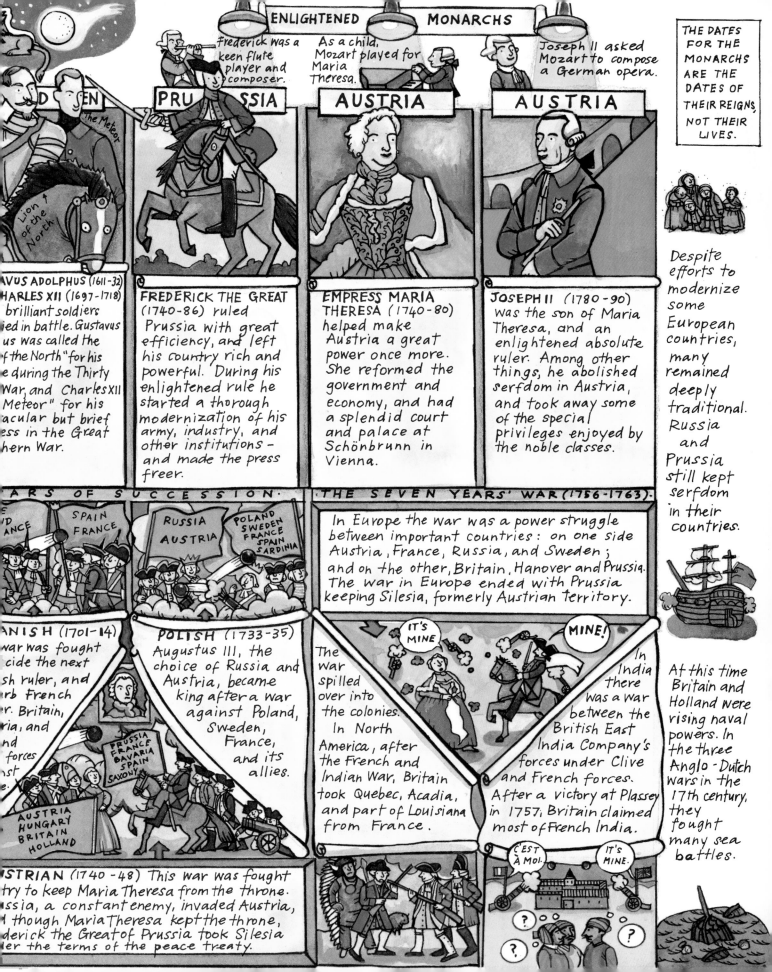

ENLIGHTENED MONARCHS

Frederick was a keen flute player and composer.

As a child, Mozart played for Maria Theresa.

Joseph II asked Mozart to compose a German opera.

THE DATES FOR THE MONARCHS ARE THE DATES OF THEIR REIGNS, NOT THEIR LIVES.

[SWE]DEN

...VUS ADOLPHUS (1611-32)
...HARLES XII (1697-1718)
... brilliant soldiers ...ied in battle. Gustavus ...us was called the ...f the North" for his ...e during the Thirty ...War, and Charles XII ...Meteor" for his ...acular but brief ...ss in the Great ...hern War.

PRUSSIA

FREDERICK THE GREAT (1740-86) ruled Prussia with great efficiency, and left his country rich and powerful. During his enlightened rule he started a thorough modernization of his army, industry, and other institutions – and made the press freer.

AUSTRIA

EMPRESS MARIA THERESA (1740-80) helped make Austria a great power once more. She reformed the government and economy, and had a splendid court and palace at Schönbrunn in Vienna.

AUSTRIA

JOSEPH II (1780-90) was the son of Maria Theresa, and an enlightened absolute ruler. Among other things, he abolished serfdom in Austria, and took away some of the special privileges enjoyed by the noble classes.

Despite efforts to modernize some European countries, many remained deeply traditional. Russia and Prussia still kept serfdom in their countries.

[W]ARS OF SUCCESSION

[SP]ANISH (1701-14)
...war was fought ...cide the next ...sh ruler, and ...rb French ...r. Britain, ...ia, and ...d ...forces ...st

POLISH (1733-35)
Augustus III, the choice of Russia and Austria, became king after a war against Poland, Sweden, France, and its allies.

[AU]STRIAN (1740-48)
This war was fought ...try to keep Maria Theresa from the throne. ...ssia, a constant enemy, invaded Austria, ...though Maria Theresa kept the throne, ...derick the Great of Prussia took Silesia ...er the terms of the peace treaty.

THE SEVEN YEARS' WAR (1756-1763)

In Europe the war was a power struggle between important countries: on one side Austria, France, Russia, and Sweden; and on the other, Britain, Hanover and Prussia. The war in Europe ended with Prussia keeping Silesia, formerly Austrian territory.

The war spilled over into the colonies. In North America, after the French and Indian War, Britain took Quebec, Acadia, and part of Louisiana from France.

IT'S MINE

MINE!

In India there was a war between the British East India Company's forces under Clive and French forces. After a victory at Plassey in 1757, Britain claimed most of French India.

C'EST À MOI.

IT'S MINE.

?

?

At this time Britain and Holland were rising naval powers. In the three Anglo-Dutch wars in the 17th century, they fought many sea battles.

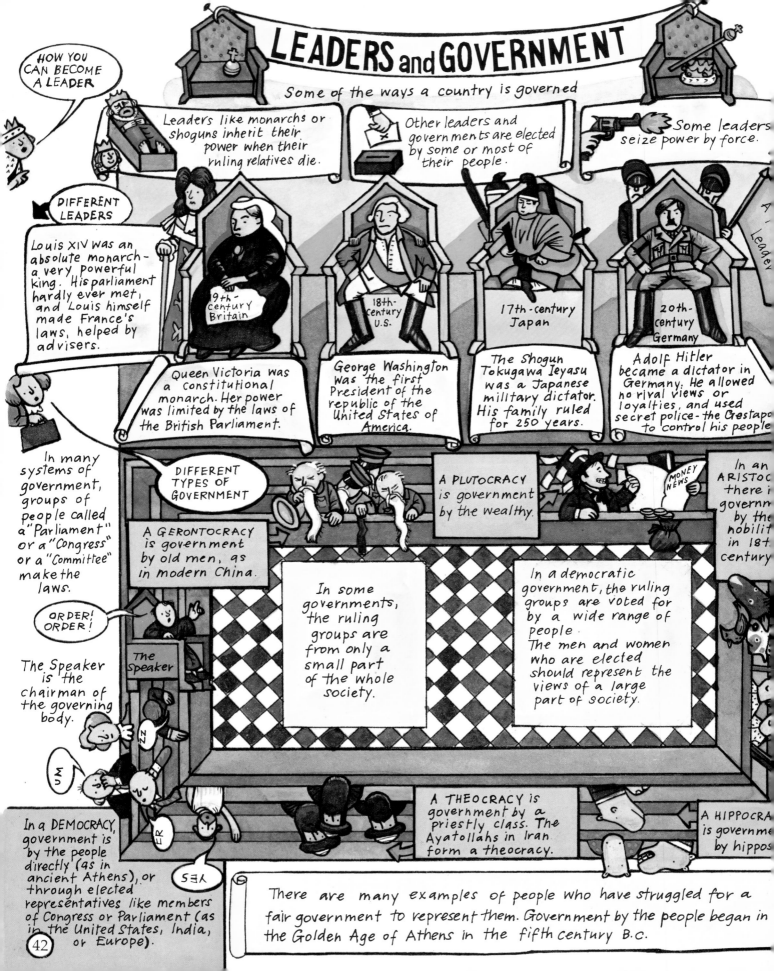

LEADERS and GOVERNMENT

Some of the ways a country is governed

HOW YOU CAN BECOME A LEADER

Leaders like monarchs or shoguns inherit their power when their ruling relatives die.

Other leaders and governments are elected by some or most of their people.

Some leaders seize power by force.

DIFFERENT LEADERS

Louis XIV was an absolute monarch - a very powerful king. His parliament hardly ever met, and Louis himself made France's laws, helped by advisers.

9th-century Britain

18th-century U.S.

17th-century Japan

20th-century Germany

A Leader

Queen Victoria was a constitutional monarch. Her power was limited by the laws of the British Parliament.

George Washington was the first President of the republic of the United States of America.

The Shogun Tokugawa Ieyasu was a Japanese military dictator. His family ruled for 250 years.

Adolf Hitler became a dictator in Germany. He allowed no rival views or loyalties, and used secret police- the Gestapo to control his people.

In many systems of government, groups of people called a "Parliament" or a "Congress" or a "Committee" make the laws.

DIFFERENT TYPES OF GOVERNMENT

A GERONTOCRACY is government by old men, as in modern China.

A PLUTOCRACY is government by the wealthy.

MONEY NEWS

In an ARISTOC there i governm by the nobilit in 18t century

ORDER! ORDER!

The Speaker is the chairman of the governing body.

The Speaker

In some governments, the ruling groups are from only a small part of the whole society.

In a democratic government, the ruling groups are voted for by a wide range of people.
The men and women who are elected should represent the views of a large part of society.

ZZ

UM

ER

In a DEMOCRACY, government is by the people directly (as in ancient Athens), or through elected representatives like members of Congress or Parliament (as in the United States, India, or Europe).

YES

A THEOCRACY is government by a priestly class. The Ayatollahs in Iran form a theocracy.

A HIPPOCRA is governme by hippos

There are many examples of people who have struggled for a fair government to represent them. Government by the people began in the Golden Age of Athens in the fifth century B.C.

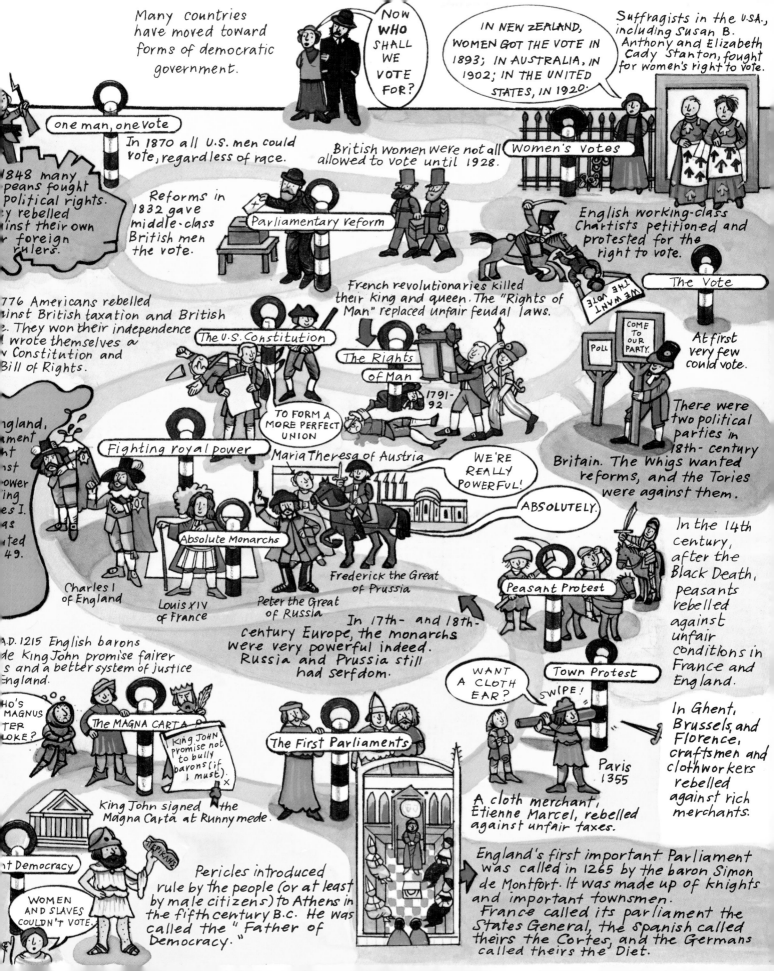

The Scientific Revolution

FRANCIS BACON (1561–1626) was one of the first men to study nature by using scientific observation. Unfortunately he died from a chill after stuffing a fowl with snow. (He was studying refrigeration.)

ATCHOO

COPERNICUS'S theory that the sun, not the earth, was at the center of the solar system was taken up by Galileo.

Galileo's apparatus to study falling bodies.

Medieval alchemists believed that God ruled the world in an unpredictable way.

SHAZAM!

After about 1600, "scientists" and philosophers began to think that man himself could use nature for his own ends, and must try to understand its laws by observation and experiment.

GALILEO GALILEI

← Galileo made paintings of the moon from observations made using his telescopes.

The two greatest figures of the scientific revoluti were Galileo and Newton. Both men studied astronom and physics.

GALILEO (1564–1642) was born in Pisa in Ital He observed the moon "seas" and mountains, the planets, and the star of the Milky Way. He also studied, using experiment ar mathematics, the laws of "falling bodies."

RAGH!

He built the first astronomical telescope studied the pendulum, and designed a clock.

Newton

NEWTON (1642–1727) was born in Lincolnshire, England, very soon after Galileo's death.

In the 1660s Newton laid the foundations of modern science. He worked on mathematical calculus, light, and gravity, and he invented his own reflecting telescope.

$$\frac{\Sigma(x_i - \bar{x})^2}{n}$$

ISAAC NEWTON

Letters between scientists of different countries

The transactions of the **ROYAL SOCIETY** and of Paris's **ACADEMY OF SCIENCES** helped spread scientific ideas.

Newton worked out laws on gravity and how things move, using observation and mathematics. He found out that white light was made up of a rainbow, or "spectrum," of colored light.

WILLIAM HARVEY

HARVEY (157 His experin and microsc observati proved th blood circulates around th body.

THE ROYAL SOCIETY

JOHN NAPIER

NAPIER (1550–1617), a Scottish mathematician, invented logarithms.

He inv a calc system u rods of ("Napier with nur on th

Galileo's compass, pendulum clock, and telescopes.

New skills in making scientific instruments like clocks, microscopes, and telescopes made really accurate observation possible for the first time.

Newton's reflecting telescope

Ro Ho comp teles

44

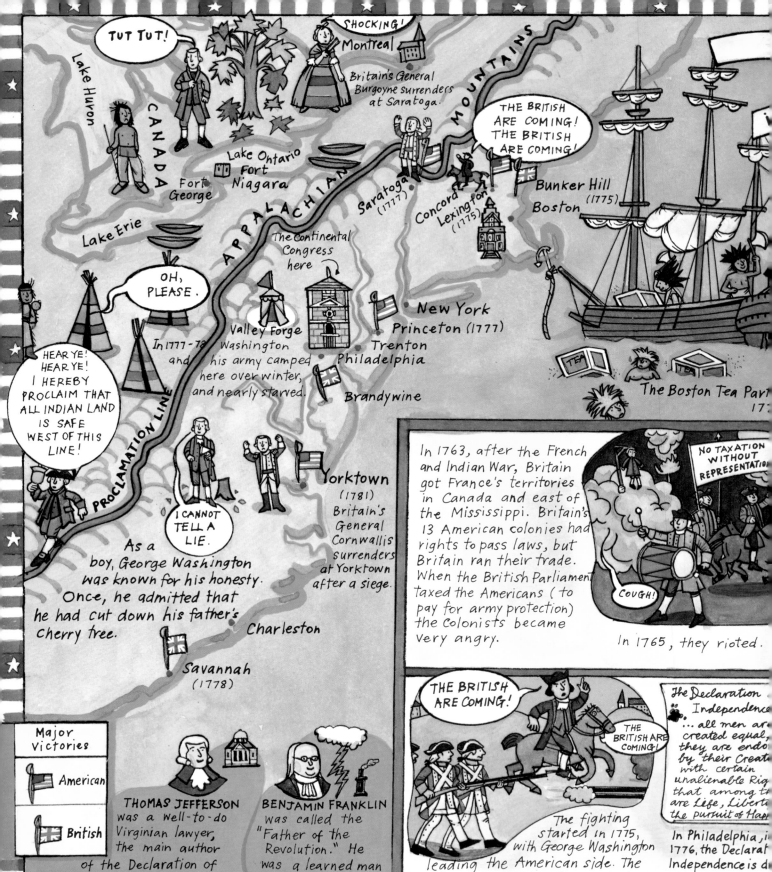

TUT TUT!

SHOCKING!
Montreal

Britain's General Burgoyne surrenders at Saratoga.

Lake Huron

CANADA

Lake Ontario
Fort Niagara

Fort George

Lake Erie

APPALACHIAN MOUNTAINS

THE BRITISH ARE COMING! THE BRITISH ARE COMING!

Saratoga (1777)

Concord
Lexington (1775)

Bunker Hill
Boston (1775)

OH, PLEASE.

The Continental Congress here

In 1777-78 Washington and his army camped here over winter, and nearly starved.

Valley Forge

New York
Princeton (1777)

Trenton
Philadelphia

Brandywine

The Boston Tea Party
17...

TEA

HEAR YE! HEAR YE! I HEREBY PROCLAIM THAT ALL INDIAN LAND IS SAFE WEST OF THIS LINE!

PROCLAMATION LINE

I CANNOT TELL A LIE.

As a boy, George Washington was known for his honesty. Once, he admitted that he had cut down his father's cherry tree.

Yorktown (1781)
Britain's General Cornwallis surrenders at Yorktown after a siege.

Charleston

Savannah (1778)

In 1763, after the French and Indian War, Britain got France's territories in Canada and east of the Mississippi. Britain's 13 American colonies had rights to pass laws, but Britain ran their trade. When the British Parliament taxed the Americans (to pay for army protection) the colonists became very angry.

NO TAXATION WITHOUT REPRESENTATION

COUGH!

In 1765, they rioted.

Major Victories

American

British

THOMAS JEFFERSON was a well-to-do Virginian lawyer, the main author of the Declaration of Independence, and the inventor of a 24-hour clock. He designed his own house, called Monticello.

BENJAMIN FRANKLIN was called the "Father of the Revolution." He was a learned man and an inventor, as well as author, editor, and printer.

THE BRITISH ARE COMING!

THE BRITISH ARE COMING!

The Declaration... Independence
... all men are created equal, they are endo... by their Creato... with certain unalienable Rig... that among t... are Life, Libert... the pursuit of Happ...

The fighting started in 1775, with George Washington leading the American side. The British were defeated in the first engagements at Lexington and Concord, because the rebels had been warned by Paul Revere.

In Philadelphia, i... 1776, the Declarat... Independence is d... and on the Four... July the Contine... Congress approv...

46

The New Machine Age

Adam Smith had a new economic theory for the factory age. He said that free market competition and free trade were best for society at large.

In the agricultural revolution before the machine age, common land was enclosed into fields.

Some landowners began to use mac and learned new of growing crops rearing animals They could proc much more food which was urgen needed in the crow citi

BAAA

Inventions like this steam threshing machine helped farmers harvest quickly and efficiently.

THE INDUSTRIAL REVOLUTION BEGAN

The railroads revolution passenger and fre trans;

Inventions were very important for the Industrial Revolution. They were exhibited in Britain's Great Exhibition and France's Exposition (1851 and 1889).

1760s

Arkwright's spinning machine

The first factories were built near rivers and used water power. Later on, factories powered by coal could be built in the growing cities where the work force lived.

In Britain, textile factories needed many workers and a lot of wool or imported cotton yarns for weaving. As long as there were good markets at home and abroad, the factory made a profit.

YES, BUT HOW DO YOU STOP

If foreign countries co not supply cotton, or mark fail fac wo co of w

THIS IS MR. JOSIAH HECKLETHWAITE, INVENTOR OF THE STOVEPIPE HAT.

Some men invested money in new inventions and businesses. These "entrepreneurs" hoped to make profits.

YOU MUST BE HARGREAVES'S SPINNING JENNY!

NO WORK!

NO PAY!

The machines could be very dangerous, especially to children, who worked long hours.

1760s Hargreaves's spinning jenny

Trevithick's steam engine

1888 Dunlop's tire

Britain's trade grew at home and abroad in the next hundred years, but Germany, the United States and Japan were close behind.

Watt's beam engine 1780s

50

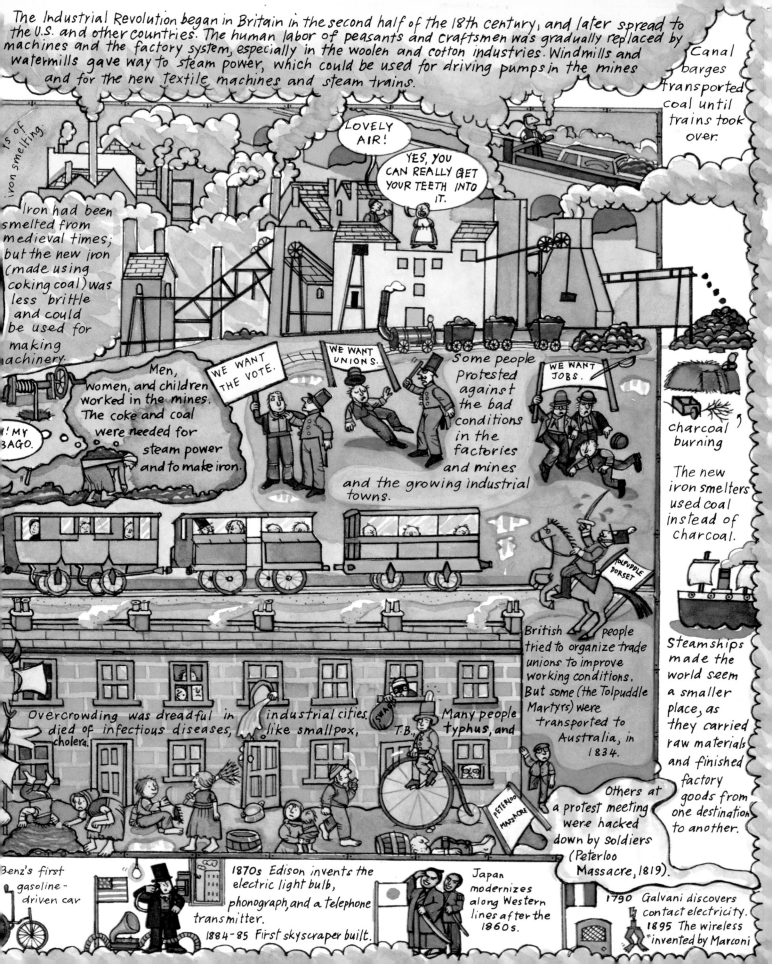

Migrants from Europe to America came in a steady stream from 1820 through 1930, peaking in the early 20th century. People left Europe in the millions to escape from hunger, hardship, or revolution in their own countries. They wanted a better future in America, the land of freedom and opportunity.

I SAY, WHERE'S THE SIDE OF THE SHIP GONE?

Most passengers were squeezed into "steerage," the space between decks. Up to 900 people had to stay there for the six-week journey.

BALTIC PEOPLES

GERMANS

POLES

RUSSIANS

CZECHS

AUSTRIANS

HUNGARIANS

ROMANIANS

→ steerage passengers

A great many people left Central and Eastern Europe.

AUSTRIA   HUNGARY   POLAND   BALKANS

ITALY   RUSSIA

The Irish potato crop failed between 1845 and 1847, and led to the death of a million people. 1,700,000 more left for the U.S. in the 1850s.

From 1880 to 1930 more than twice as many arrived. Many came from central, southern, and eastern Europe.

IRELAND   BRITAIN

In Britain there was hardship and overcrowding. A steady flow of emigrants left in the 19th century.

COLLECTION POINT

Train passengers from all over Europe gathered at collection points.

Early emigrants went to America on board wooden sailing ships. Iron steamships, like this one, the Great Eastern, carried passengers – up to 4000. Unfortunately, ship rolled very badly, and it was scrapped.

Between 1788 and 1868, the British government "transported" convicts to newly discovered Australia.

Emigrants were ferried out to their ships.

EMBARK HERE

At the embarkation point the emigrants were bathed, fumigated, had their papers checked, and paid the $25 for their passage.

CRIKEY, IT'S A TUNNEL!

HOW EMBARRASSING.

YOUR PAPERS, SIR?

People left their homelands for many reasons.

REVOLUTION IN EUROPE

AMBITION TO GET ON IN THE WORLD

ATTACKS ON JEWS IN RUSSIA

FAMINE IN IRELAND

FOR ADVENTURE

Women and men traveled in separate boxcars in parts of Europe.

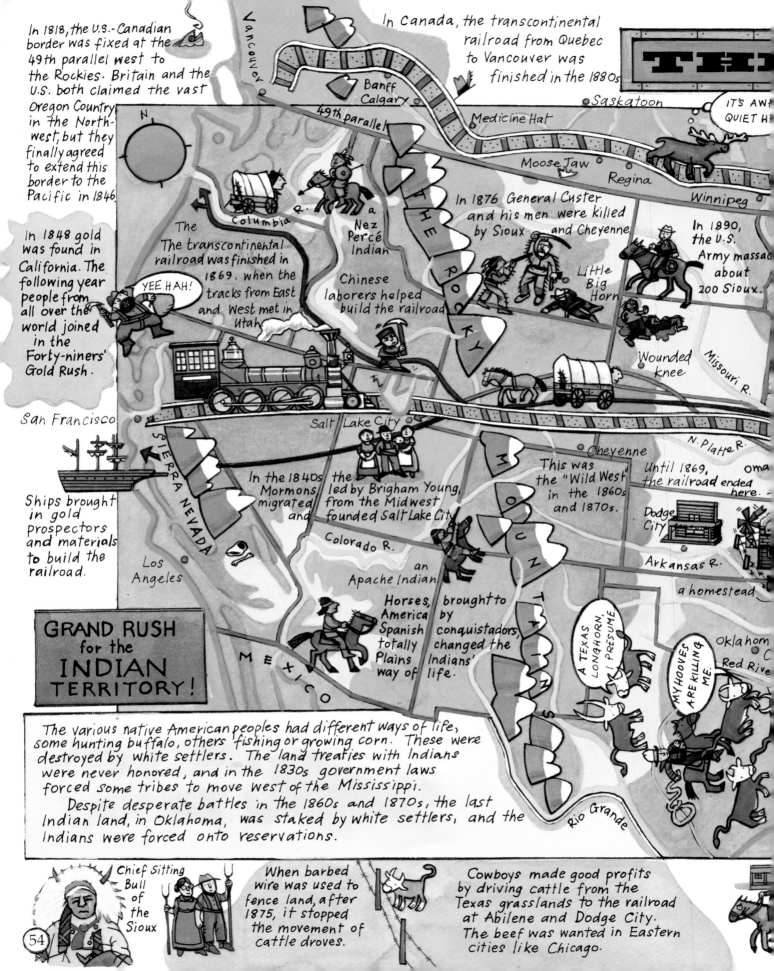

In 1818, the U.S.-Canadian border was fixed at the 49th parallel west to the Rockies. Britain and the U.S. both claimed the vast Oregon Country in the Northwest, but they finally agreed to extend this border to the Pacific in 1846.

In Canada, the transcontinental railroad from Quebec to Vancouver was finished in the 1880s

In 1848 gold was found in California. The following year people from all over the world joined in the Forty-niners' Gold Rush.

The transcontinental railroad was finished in 1869, when the tracks from East and West met in Utah.

Chinese laborers helped build the railroad

In 1876 General Custer and his men were killed by Sioux and Cheyenne

In 1890, the U.S. Army massac about 200 Sioux.

Ships brought in gold prospectors and materials to build the railroad.

In the 1840s the Mormons, led by Brigham Young, migrated from the Midwest and founded Salt Lake City.

This was the "Wild West" in the 1860s and 1870s.

Until 1869, the railroad ended here.

Horses, brought to America by Spanish conquistadors, totally changed the Plains Indians' way of life.

GRAND RUSH for the INDIAN TERRITORY!

The various native American peoples had different ways of life, some hunting buffalo, others fishing or growing corn. These were destroyed by white settlers. The land treaties with Indians were never honored, and in the 1830s government laws forced some tribes to move west of the Mississippi.

Despite desperate battles in the 1860s and 1870s, the last Indian land, in Oklahoma, was staked by white settlers, and the Indians were forced onto reservations.

Chief Sitting Bull of the Sioux

When barbed wire was used to fence land, after 1875, it stopped the movement of cattle droves.

Cowboys made good profits by driving cattle from the Texas grasslands to the railroad at Abilene and Dodge City. The beef was wanted in Eastern cities like Chicago.

54

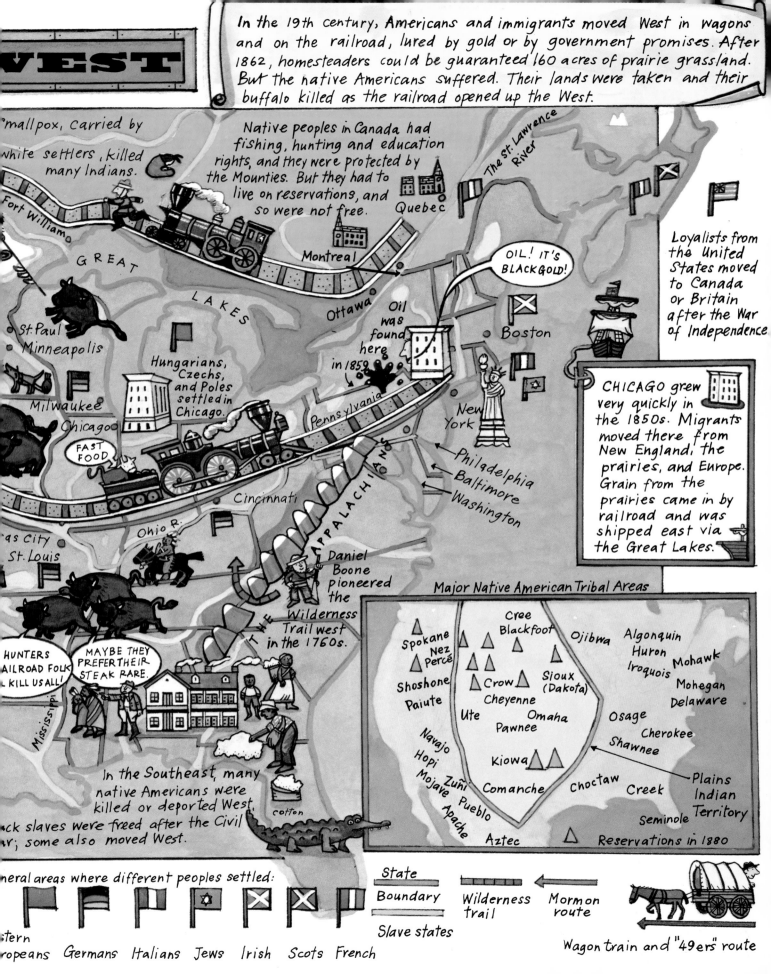

WEST

In the 19th century, Americans and immigrants moved West in wagons and on the railroad, lured by gold or by government promises. After 1862, homesteaders could be guaranteed 160 acres of prairie grassland. But the native Americans suffered. Their lands were taken and their buffalo killed as the railroad opened up the West.

...mallpox, carried by white settlers, killed many Indians.

Native peoples in Canada had fishing, hunting and education rights, and they were protected by the Mounties. But they had to live on reservations, and so were not free.

Quebec

Montreal

Ottawa

The St. Lawrence River

OIL! IT'S BLACK GOLD!

Oil was found here in 1859

Boston

New York

Loyalists from the United States moved to Canada or Britain after the War of Independence

GREAT LAKES

Fort William

St. Paul
Minneapolis

Hungarians, Czechs, and Poles settled in Chicago.

Milwaukee
Chicago

FAST FOOD

Pennsylvania

Philadelphia
Baltimore
Washington

CHICAGO grew very quickly in the 1850s. Migrants moved there from New England, the prairies, and Europe. Grain from the prairies came in by railroad and was shipped east via the Great Lakes.

Cincinnati

Ohio R.

...as City
St. Louis

APPALACHIANS

Daniel Boone pioneered the Wilderness Trail west in the 1760s.

Major Native American Tribal Areas

THE

HUNTERS
...AILROAD FOLK
...KILL US ALL!

MAYBE THEY PREFER THEIR STEAK RARE.

In the Southeast, many native Americans were killed or deported West.
...ck slaves were freed after the Civil ...ar; some also moved West.

cotton

Spokane
Nez Percé
Shoshone
Paiute

Cree
Blackfoot

Crow
Cheyenne
Ute
Pawnee
Omaha

Sioux (Dakota)

Ojibwa

Algonquin
Huron
Iroquois
Mohawk
Mohegan
Delaware

Osage
Cherokee
Shawnee

Navajo
Hopi
Mojave Zuñi
Apache
Pueblo
Aztec

Kiowa
Comanche

Choctaw

Creek

Seminole

Plains Indian Territory

Reservations in 1880

...neral areas where different peoples settled:

...stern
...ropeans
Germans
Italians
Jews
Irish
Scots
French

State
Boundary
Slave states

Wilderness trail

Mormon route

Wagon train and "49ers" route

In the early 19th century, most of Africa was made up of independent African kingdoms.

THE SCRAMBLE FOR AFRICA

THE WHITE GRA...

As the Ottoman Empire weakened, the French began to take an interest in its North African territories.

Algeria was conquered by the French in 1830.

At this time most of Africa south of the Sahara was unknown to Europeans, except for coastal trading posts. Even there, many white men died of malaria. They hardly ever traveled far the inland, where conditions we even worse. African tra had to br their go to the instea

Tangier
Algeria
Tunis
Morocco
Tripoli
Cyrenaica
Cairo
Fezzan
Egypt
Nile R.
Red Sea
Nubia

Caravans, or companies of Arab merchants, crossed the Sahara with their camel trains.

WATER!
SORRY, I'M A MIRAGE.

The Sahara

An Arab Caravan

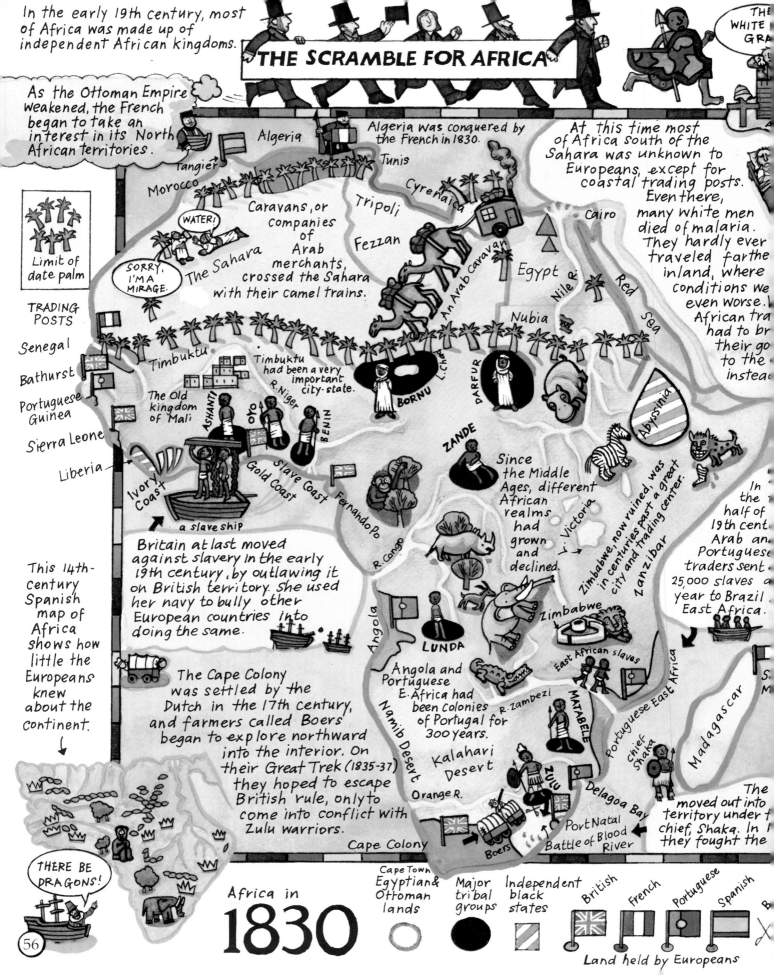

Limit of date palm

TRADING POSTS

Senegal
Bathurst
Portuguese Guinea
Sierra Leone
Liberia

Timbuktu

Timbuktu had been a very important city-state.

The Old kingdom of Mali

ASHANTI
OYO
BENIN
R. Niger

BORNU
L. Chad
DARFUR
ZANDE
Abyssinia

Ivory Coast
Gold Coast
Slave Coast
Fernando Po
a slave ship

Britain at last moved against slavery in the early 19th century, by outlawing it on British territory. She used her navy to bully other European countries into doing the same.

Since the Middle Ages, different African realms had grown and declined.

Zimbabwe, now ruined, was in centuries past a great city and trading center.

L. Victoria

Zanzibar

In the half of 19th cent Arab an Portuguese traders sent 25,000 slaves a year to Brazil East Africa.

R. Congo

This 14th-century Spanish map of Africa shows how little the Europeans knew about the continent.

Angola
LUNDA
Zimbabwe
R. Zambezi
MATABELE
East African slaves
Portuguese East Africa
Madagascar

The Cape Colony was settled by the Dutch in the 17th century, and farmers called Boers began to explore northward into the interior. On their Great Trek (1835-37) they hoped to escape British rule, only to come into conflict with Zulu warriors.

Angola and Portuguese E. Africa had been colonies of Portugal for 300 years.

Namib Desert
Kalahari Desert
Orange R.
ZULU
chief Shaka
Delagoa Bay

The moved out into territory under f chief, Shaka. In t they fought the

THERE BE DRAGONS!

Cape Colony
Boers
Port Natal
Battle of Blood River

Africa in

1830

Cape Town

Egyptian & Ottoman lands

Major tribal groups

Independent black states

British   French   Portuguese   Spanish   B

Land held by Europeans

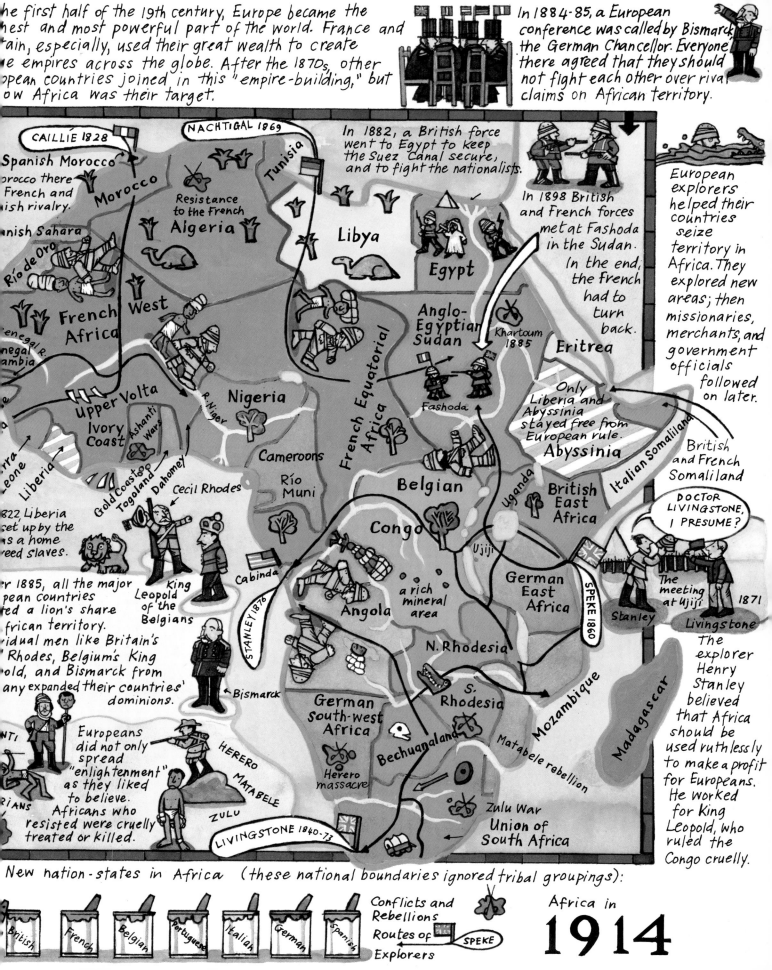

...he first half of the 19th century, Europe became the ...hest and most powerful part of the world. France and ...tain, especially, used their great wealth to create ...e empires across the globe. After the 1870s, other ...opean countries joined in this "empire-building," but ...ow Africa was their target.

In 1884-85, a European conference was called by Bismarck, the German Chancellor. Everyone there agreed that they should not fight each other over rival claims on African territory.

CAILLIE 1828

NACHTIGAL 1869

Spanish Morocco
...orocco there
...French and
...ish rivalry.

...nish Sahara

Río de Oro

Morocco

Resistance to the French
Algeria

Tunisia

Libya

In 1882, a British force went to Egypt to keep the Suez Canal secure, and to fight the nationalists.

Egypt

In 1898 British and French forces met at Fashoda in the Sudan. In the end, the French had to turn back.

European explorers helped their countries seize territory in Africa. They explored new areas; then missionaries, merchants, and government officials followed on later.

...negal R.
...ambia

French West Africa

Upper Volta
Ivory Coast
Ashanti Wars

...rra ... Leone
Liberia

Anglo-Egyptian Sudan

Khartoum 1885

Fashoda

Eritrea

Only Liberia and Abyssinia stayed free from European rule.

Abyssinia

Italian Somaliland

British and French Somaliland

R. Niger
Nigeria

Cameroons

French Equatorial Africa

Río Muni

...822 Liberia
...et up by the
...s a home
...eed slaves.

Gold Coast
Togoland
Dahomey

Cecil Rhodes

King Leopold of the Belgians

Cabinda

STANLEY 1876

Angola

a rich mineral area

Belgian
Congo

Ujiji

Uganda

British East Africa

German East Africa

SPEKE 1860

DOCTOR LIVINGSTONE, I PRESUME?

The meeting at Ujiji
1871

Stanley

Livingstone

...r 1885, all the major
...pean countries
...ted a lion's share
...frican territory.
...idual men like Britain's
... Rhodes, Belgium's King
...old, and Bismarck from
...any expanded their countries'
dominions.

Bismarck

Europeans did not only spread "enlightenment" as they liked to believe. Africans who resisted were cruelly treated or killed.

...NTI
...RIANS

HERERO
MATABELE
ZULU

German south-west Africa

Herero massacre

Bechuanaland

Matabele rebellion

N. Rhodesia

S. Rhodesia

Mozambique

Madagascar

Zulu War
Union of South Africa

LIVINGSTONE 1840-73

The explorer Henry Stanley believed that Africa should be used ruthlessly to make a profit for Europeans. He worked for King Leopold, who ruled the Congo cruelly.

New nation-states in Africa (these national boundaries ignored tribal groupings):

British   French   Belgian   Portuguese   Italian   German   Spanish

Conflicts and Rebellions

Routes of Explorers

SPEKE

Africa in

1914

THE VICTORIAN AGE

An age, most unusually, named after a monarch, was not found only in Britain.

The Queen gave her name to many places in her empire.

VICTORIA became the British queen in 1837, and she reigned until 1901. In those 64 years there were tremendous changes in Britain and its growing empire, as well as in Europe and the Americas.

British industry made mementos, now called Victoriana, for her Jubilees.

VICTORIA

EMPIRES

In 1885, near the end of the Victorian Age, some European countries had a "Scramble" for African land. They said it was the White Man's Burden to govern and educate the Africans...

...but they also wanted new territories, markets, and cheap raw materials.

FOREIGN PLACES

Some isolationist countries like China and Japan did not like foreigners at all. Japan was forced to open up to American trade in 1854.

In Europe itself, the balance of power was changing, and some countries were at war. CRIMEA 1854-56, ITALY 1859-61, PRUSSIA 1860s-1870s

France, Britain, and Turkey defeated Russia.

Italy won unity and freedom from Austria.

Bismarck helped Prussia become strong, and later he led a united Germany.

REVOLUTION

1848 was the Year of Revolutions in Europe. Some people protested about food shortages. Others, called nationalists, wanted to get rid of foreign rulers.

In 1848 Marx and Engels wrote the Communist Manifesto.

ELECTORAL REFORM

In Britain, only men chose which political party governed under Victoria, the constitutional monarch. Reforms in 1867 and 1884 let more men vote but not women.

New Zealand women got the vote in 1893.

PLEASINGLY ENTERTAINING WRITERS & MUSICIANS

Verdi   Gounod   Wagner   Trollope   Dickens   Edward Lear

AMAZING SCIENTIFIC DISCOVERIES

Darwin, Pasteur, and the Curies were among the great scientists of the Victorian Age.

Darwin devised the theory of evolution.

Pasteur devised the germ theory of disease.

The Curies discovered radium, an element later used in x-ray therapy.

The standard of living improved a lot for the working class over the years from 1837 to 1901. But there were very bad times, too.

THE WORKSHOP OF THE WORLD

Industrialization turned Victorian England into "workshop of the world."

THIS IS PROGRESS?

GREAT EXHIBITION

ENGLAND

OH, WHY DID I BECOME A WINDOW CLEANER?

The huge glass building housed the Great Exhibition in 1851. It showed off the products of British, European, and American industry.

MAGNIFICENT VICTORIAN WHISKERS

Bismarck, Queen Victoria, Garibaldi, Reuter, Mutton chop, Marx, Gladstone, W.G. Grace (cricketer), Florence Nightingale

Fashionable whiskers included the famous mutton-chop.

CLASS

Victorian England had a very strong class system.

RIFF-RAFF!
TOFFS!
THEY'RE SO COMMON.

UPPER CLASS
MIDDLE CLASS
WORKING CLASS

FEARFUL POVERTY

The 1840s were bad times for poor people. In Britain they were called the Hungry Forties. If people had no money or work, they could be sent into workhouses.

THE HARVEST HAS FAILED.
I CAN'T AFFORD BREAD.
THE FACTORY HAS FIRED ME.

In Ireland a potato blight in 1845 caused a famine which killed around a million people.

In Europe, in 1848, hungry people called for revolution.

GO WEST!

To escape slums, poverty, and hunger, and to look for freedom and fortune, people left

THERE'S GOLD IN THEM THAR HILLS.

Europe for America. Some joined the Gold Rush to California, after gold was found there in 1848.

TRANSPORTATION

Some British convicts were forced to serve their sentence in Australia. This "transportation" lasted until 1868.

NO ONE ASKED US.

VICTORIAN VALUES

Victorians were known for certain values.

DUTY
LEND US A HAND, MA'AM.
Florence Nightingale in the Crimea

CHARITY
In America, Carnegie gave money for education.

DISCIPLINE
5 COLD BATHS A DAY...
THAT'S HOW I GOT WHERE I AM!

HARD WORK and SELF-RELIANCE
HARD WORK NEVER HARMED ANYONE!
I WOULDN'T LIKE TO RISK IT.

WOMEN
CHILDREN
MEN

The workhouse

Other Victorian transportation

Brunel's Great Western Railway

At the beginning of the 20th century, a few European countries were the major world powers. They had large empires and great wealth.

The Twentieth Century

Oh dear, DEPRE...

There have been many changes since 1900. Inventions, especially, have affected many areas of life.

Micro-computers and electronic calculators

Industrial robots, lasers, and oxy-acetylene equipment

Scientific inventions

The electron microscope and radio telescopes

1900 - 1909

Queen Victoria dies, ending the Victorian era.
CROAK!

IN THE AIR
The first Zeppelin airship flies!
1900

The first powered flight by the Wright brothers 1903

The Cubist movement in art
PICASSO PAINTED THIS.

The first radio transmission between the U.S. and Britain

Suffragists protest in the U.S. and Britain.
VOTES FOR WOMEN
UNHAND ME, OFFICER!

1910 - 1919

Lenin
COMMUNISM
END PRIVATE OWNERSHIP!
Communists take over in the Russian Revolution.

WORLD WAR I 1914 - 1918
fought between Germany and the Allies to maintain Europe's balance of power.

The sinking of the Titanic
1912

$E = mc^2$ Einstein's theory of relativity

WELL, IT MAKES YOU THINK.
FREUD'S work on Psycho-analysis

THE TWENTIES

BROTHER, CAN YOU SPARE A DIME?
The Wall Street Crash: U.S. stocks fall. 1929.

Stalin takes over in the U.S.S.R. and he industrializes Russia.
MILLIONS DIE IN MY REIGN OF TERROR.

LINDBERGH
The first solo Atlantic crossing in 1927

I DISCOVER PENICILLIN IN 1928.
FLEMING

Prohibition of alcohol in the U.S. causes gangsterism.

JAZZ POPULAR IN THE U.S.
AL JOLSON
1927 Jolson's "The Jazz Singer" is the first film "talkie"
THAT'S ANOTHER FINE MESS.

The early days of Hollywood

Ford's mass-produced cars

Gandhi uses non-violence to campaign for Indian independence.

THE THIRTIE[S]

A NEW DEAL
The Great Depression: U.S. President Franklin D. Roosevelt tries to end the economic crisis.

In China, the "Long March" is led by the Communist leader Ma[o] Tse-tung. 1934 - 35.

R101
Airship disasters R101 (1930) and Hindenburg (1937)

The first paperback boo[k]

The Wizard of Oz
1939
Hollywood films become very po[pular]

FASCISM
Franco (Spain), Hit[ler] (Germany), and Musse[lini] (Italy) are dictators

I INVAD[E] POLAN[D] IN 193[9]
Hitler starts World War I[I]

Teflon →
Labor-saving household equipment

Medical inventions
Electrocardiographs and dialysis equipment

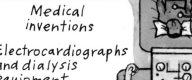

New forms of Communication and transport

COPIERS
TELEX

FAX   TV

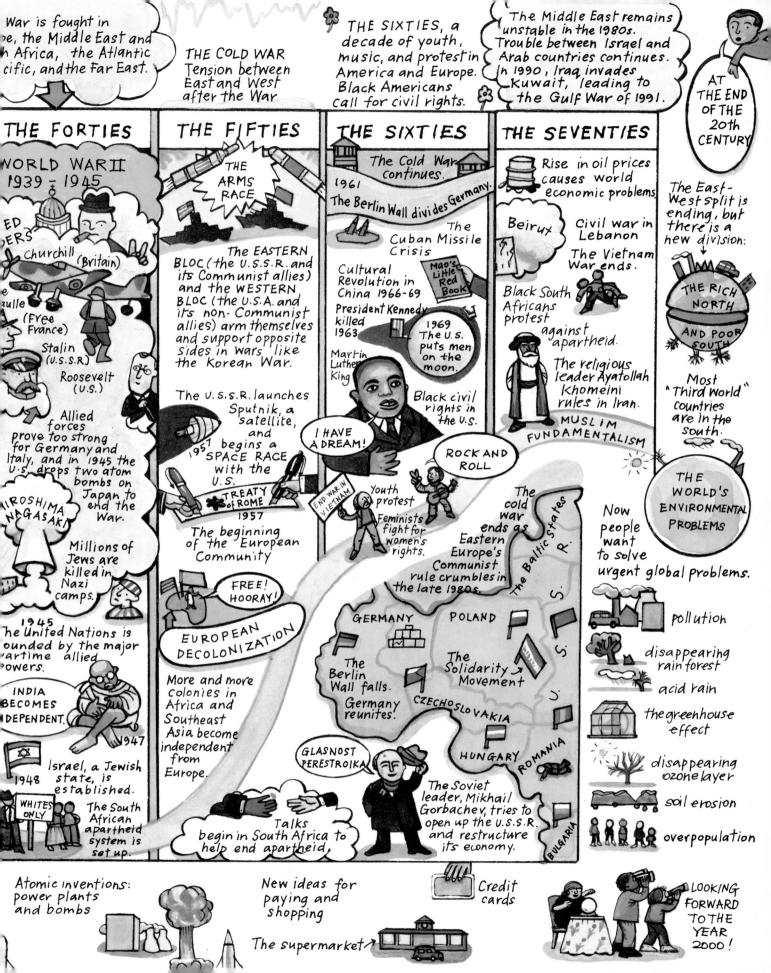

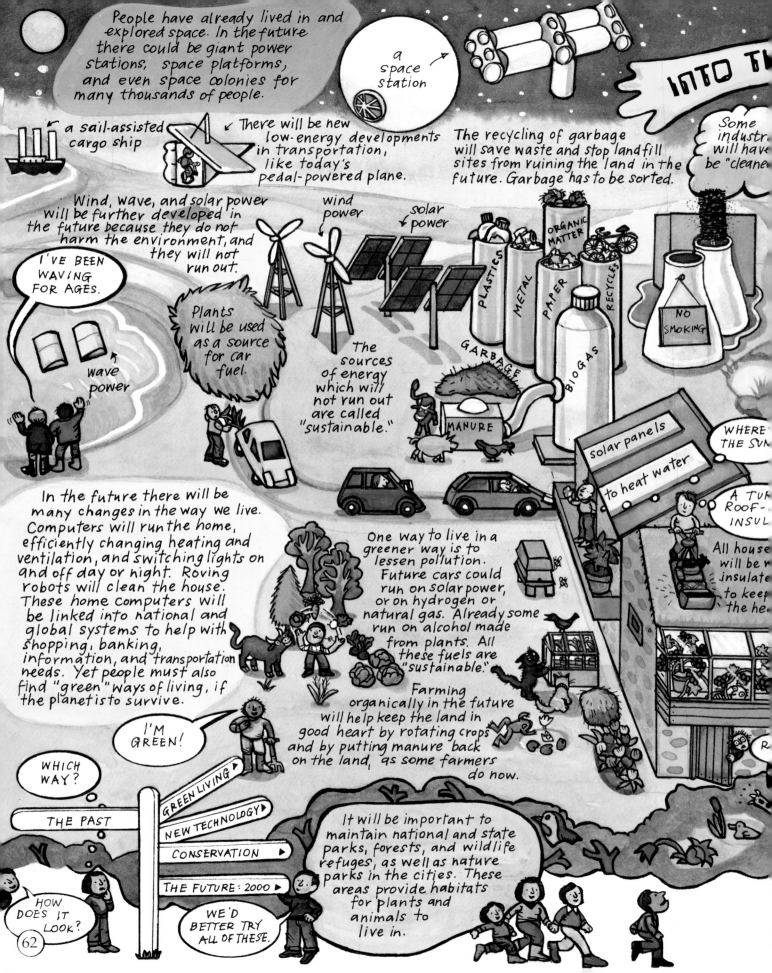

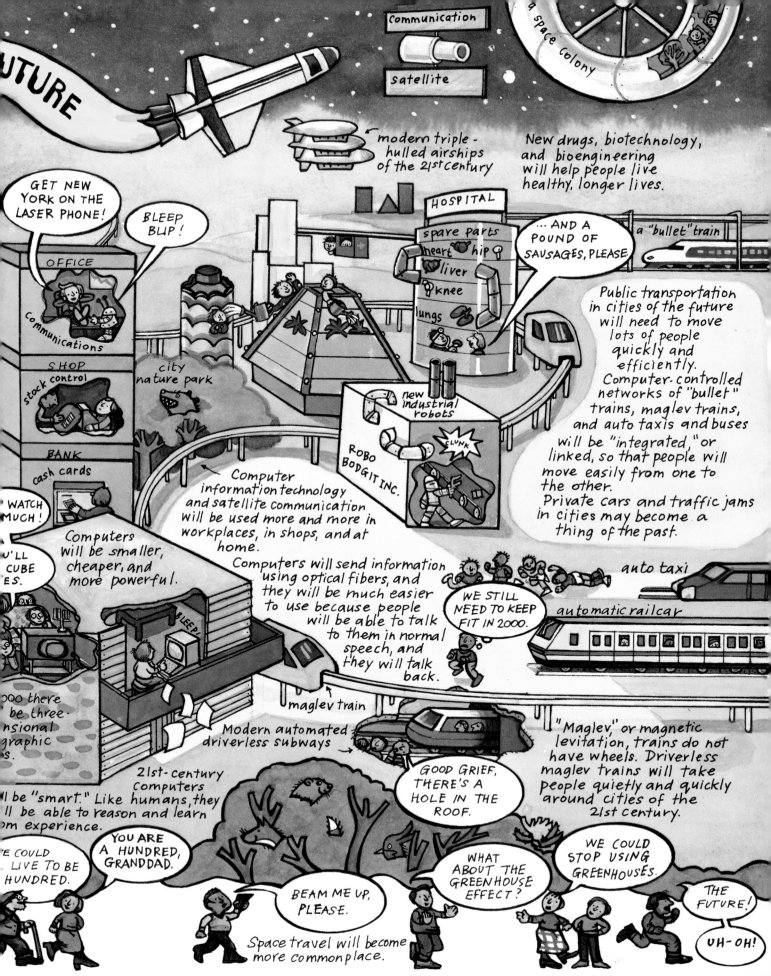